Nice Guys Can Win!

Wesley Harris

Wrightbooks

By the same author:
Battlelines

Acknowledgements:
Thanks to **John Smith** for
permission to include his photographs
throughout the book.

First published in 1995. Reprinted 1996

Wrightbooks Pty Ltd
PO Box 270
Elsternwick
Victoria 3185

ACN 007 050 277

Ph: (03) 9532 7082
Fax: (03) 9532 7084

National Library of Australia
Cataloguing-in-publication data:

Harris, Wesley.
  Nice Guys Can Win!
  ISBN 1 875857 12 5
  1. Self-actualization (Psychology). 2. Success -
  Psychological aspects. I. Title.
158.1
Cover design by Rob Cowpe
Printed in Australia by Griffin Paperbacks

ISBN: 1 875857 12 5

Contents

Dedication

To Peter
my son—and a nice guy!

Preface

IT MAY HAVE been a rather corny comic who quipped, 'As the mosquito said when it hit the windscreen, 'I didn't know I had that much in me!' More seriously, none of us knows how much we have in us, good or bad. Potentially, there is bad in the best of us and good in the worst of us.

So which part of us is to be cultivated if we are to be winners?

There is an American expression which has variations around the world. It goes something like this: 'Nice guys don't win' or 'Good guys come last'. The thought is that it is necessary to be a bit of a 'baddie' in order to be successful. In that case what do you stop at—murder? Can you only climb to success over the corpses of your competitors—even metaphorically speaking? Shouldn't we leave the rat race to rats and stay with the human race instead?

Competition may be good but must it be cut-throat? In order to rise must we put others down? To be a winner must we inevitably make others losers? Or can we aim for 'win-win' results?

My contention is that you can be a 'nice guy' and a winner and I propose to cite many factual, up-to-date examples to prove my point. But first, I need to define my terms.

When I refer to 'guys' I mean people of both sexes. Time was when only males were referred to as guys. Not any more! When we lived in North America my wife and I had to get used to being referred to as 'youse guys'.

Then when I refer to a 'nice guy' I am not just thinking of the kind of person who can't say 'no' even when that would be the right answer. I am certainly not thinking of the man or woman who will promise the moon—even if that celestial body doesn't happen to be part of their stock in trade. I am thinking rather of the sort of person who is known to be 'fair dinkum' and who, apart from anything else, has some concern for other people.

Then what about winning?

Is that only a matter of dollars and cents? Is a dollar sign big enough to measure the world? Well, of course money matters. None of us can get far without it. 'The golden rule is that gold rules', says the cynic, and sometimes we may concede that he has a point.

This book will tell of people whose winnings could be counted in lots of dollars and cents but I contend that they have been financial winners largely because they have been nice guys and not in spite of that fact. Their Midas touch has come from their human touch. Being people-sensitive has made them successful.

But are rich people the only winners? If they are then people like Mother Teresa must be losers and few would say that. Might not what people *give* be an even better indication of being winners than what they *get?*

Then winning in one area of life has to be balanced against the cost of losing in another.

For example, if a man succeeds in business at the cost of his marriage and with the loss of his family is he a winner?

This book will not only probe such conundrums but will seek to come up with some answers to the question of how to be a winner—in the broadest sense of the term. Many of the answers have been hammered out on the hard anvil of experience. They are certainly not untried or airy fairy theories. So let's look at them together!

Wesley Harris
Melbourne, August 1995

Chapter One

Go For Goal!

A CARTOON depicted two men from Mars approaching planet Earth. They could see people hurrying and scurrying here and there. One Martian said to the other:

'What are they doing?'

His companion replied:

'They are going?' '

But,' said the first, *'where are they going?'*

'Oh,' came the reply, *'they are not going anywhere. They are just going'.*

That may be a picture of many in our helter-skelter generation whose lives are characterised by perpetual motion with no real direction.

Football fans would have little patience with players who ran on to the field and were like puppies chasing their own tails instead of going for goal. The derisive cries of the crowd would not be hard to imagine. Yet perhaps many of the spectators would themselves lack any real sense of direction in their lives. Winners on the sports field are people who know where and what their goal is—and go for it. And the same applies in almost any field of activity. Greg Norman says:

'Better golf is not just a title; it's a personal goal'.

Johnny Weismuller took the main role in the *Tarzan* films familiar to an earlier generation. He broke 67 swimming records and told of some advice he received when he was a youngster. As a swimmer he was losing valuable time through not keeping a straight course. One day his coach placed a hat on the spring-

1

board at one end of the pool. 'That is your goal' he shouted. 'Fix it in your mind. Draw a mental line and swim for it.'

Weismuller reckoned that this advice took him through two sets of Olympic Games in which he won five medals. And he said that, apart from swimming, he always tried to keep a goal in life.

It might surprise some to know that St Paul took an interest in the sporting life of his time. With reference to his own particular calling—but with the image of a First Century equivalent of our own Australian Kathy Freeman in mind—he wrote:

> *'Forgetting what is behind and straining toward what is ahead, I press on toward the goal...'*

The same image might appeal to us and be related to our particular circumstances.

One of the biggest construction firms in the United Kingdom is called WIMPEY. Its name is derived from the initials of the words in its slogan:

> *We Intend Making Progress Every Year.*

Now of course, that would be a worthy goal for any individual or group of people, but how to achieve it is something else. Sheer hard work is one way!

Mal is now a successful plastic surgeon in Victoria, Australia. As long as he can remember he has wanted to be a doctor. At 13 he was taken to a plastic surgeon for a minor procedure. Later, when he saw the doctor driving away in his Jaguar he knew exactly what he wanted to be when he grew up!

(Years later the same surgeon was Mal's examiner and was delighted to learn that he had inspired one small boy — not only with his car but with his profession.)

The trouble was that, as Mal concedes, he was only a little above average academically. However, at school he studied early and late. It was therefore a great disappointment that in his final school exams his marks were not high enough to get him into a medical faculty. He managed to get into a science course and three years in succession failed to get a transfer to medicine. With a science degree he thought he would try pharmacy but his heart was not in it.

Then, out of the blue, came the offer of a place in medicine. Eventually he got his medical degree and decided that surgery was still what he wanted. However, clawing his way up his chosen mountain was still not easy. Only at his third attempt did he pass the difficult entrance exam. During a period in England he met his future wife, a nurse, in an operating theatre. Following marriage he returned to Australia and sat his final examinations three times before passing. His story is one of sheer determination and discipline.

Talking to the now successful Mal, I quoted R.L. Stevenson:

'To travel hopefully is better than to arrive'.

To arrive may be to stagnate. So I asked whether he had *'arrived'*. 'No way.' he said, 'At the beginning of every year I set new goals and at the beginning of each week I set goals'.

Mal strikes a careful balance between his dedication to his beloved profession, his wife and children and his church involvement and seems a happy man.

What about Goal Setting?

There are three important things to remember when setting goals.

First, the goals need to be challenging. I once asked a man in middle management about his goals for the work under his direction. I got the impression that he wasn't keen on having goals for fear that he wouldn't achieve them. However, after a little persuasion he did set out some goals, but they barely exceeded the status quo, although in fact there was plenty of scope for improvement. Meaningful goals should challenge us not only to 'do our best' but to do 'better than our best' and surpass our previous achievements.

Then goals need to be achievable. I recall a fellow whose optimism and enthusiasm made him an endearing personality. He liked to build castles in the air—which in a sense is where castles need to be. The trouble was that he didn't always count the cost of putting foundations under his castles. For that reason, some of his plans never came to anything. In setting goals we need to be realistic and ready to make every effort to reach them. John Calvin is reported to have said:

'Faith can move mountains - faith and a spade'.

Then ideally, goals should be specific and measurable. Some people like to have their goals enveloped in the mist of generalities so that any failure to score will not be too obvious. For example, they may say that their goal is to have a better spirit in the office which could be both desirable and necessary. But deciding whether or not such a goal has been reached may be very much a matter of subjective judgement. There needs to be practical evidence of the better spirit shown, for example, in improved productivity, punctuality or whatever.

Before goals are effective they have to be accepted. It is said that good goals are *my* goals and bad goals are *your* goals. There's a point there. A prime task of leadership is to get other people to accept and own worthy goals.

President Dwight Eisenhower said:

'Leadership is to get people to do what you want because they want to'.

This is more likely to work by drawing people than by driving them. Just as a length of string cannot be pushed only pulled so it is with people, very often.

Groups or individuals need to have both long-term and short-term goals with some correlation between them. It might be good to write a couple of sentences indicating life goals and then in the light of them put down in black and white, goals for each of the next five years as well as objectives for the immediate future. (Incidentally, writing down our aims and objectives makes them more concrete in our thinking and helps us in a regular review of our situation and in honest monitoring of progress made.)

When I retired after living a very busy and focused life, I realised that I might be in danger of drifting and losing sight of purposeful aims that would enable me to keep the zest in living. For that reason, setting down meaningful long-term goals was important, together with aims for every day.

Get a Round Tuit

A notice in an office posed the question, 'Have you got a round tuit?' It probably caused a few smiles but hopefully it also stirred to action people who, while meaning well, might otherwise never have got around to doing what needed to be done.

Procrastination is a problem for some people. Their motto seems to be, 'Never do today what can be done tomorrow'—and sometimes it seems that tomorrow never comes.

I recall that when I was a young man my friends and I used to joke about the LBW file. (It should be said that LBW did not denote 'leg before wicket' but 'Let the Beggars Wait!') Into that file went some Head Office requests for information and other matters of inconvenience. I haven't heard of an LBW file for years. Maybe it has gone out of fashion, or perhaps it is called by another name!

Reasonably early, probably to the relief of my superiors, I must have had a kind of Damascus road experience and seen the light, for I found that the motto, 'Do it now!' had much more to commend it!

Without becoming obsessive, I have made a habit through the years of setting myself reasonable time limits for finishing tasks such as completing a writing assignment or mowing the lawn or whatever. Unexpected interruptions have sometimes prevented completion of tasks on time but often the self-imposed deadline has concentrated the mind and aided achievement. Of course, other people operate differently; I simply record what has worked for me.

The Ten Commandments not only include the wise provision for a day of rest but a 'time and motion' programme for the completion of tasks.

> *'Remember the Sabbath day by keeping it holy. Six days you shall labour and do all your work'.*

It is not just what we do but what we get done that counts.

The best goal getters are usually goal setters. While it may sometimes be good for others to set goals for us, the most stimulating goals could be those we set for ourselves. Providing those goals are worthy, striving for them will draw the very best out of us. We need to believe to achieve. If we are convinced that what we are working for is worthwhile, then when the going is tough we will be buoyed up by imagining the thrill of achievement which awaits us.

So We Go For Goal!

Reaching the goal is our 'magnificent obsession'. Worthwhile achievement is the name of our game, and for that no sacrifice is too great.

Chapter Two

Winners Need a Sense of Proportion

WORRY is the interest we pay on tomorrow's troubles and it is often at an extortionate rate—particularly as some of the troubles never actually eventuate and others are not such a big deal anyway. But worrying about them may be no small matter. We may lie awake at night, sick with anxiety, burning up nervous energy we should be conserving for the work of the following day. Perhaps the need is to develop a sense of proportion.

Mothers-in-law are often the butt of jokes and I confess that I used to tease my mother-in-law on occasion, although I appreciated her very much. She was a wise, somewhat matter-of-fact woman who served for many years as a missionary in China and then worked in Czechoslovakia until the Communist regime came to power. She had known a great deal of sorrow as well as joy and had developed her own special philosophy of life.

Sometimes, if I was fretting about something or other, she would smile at me and say, 'Don't worry, it will make no difference in a hundred years from now'. In other words, she was advising me to look at the concern of the moment in the context of the long term. Winners must be able to do that.

Robert Schuller said:

> *'Tough times never last, but tough people do'.*

We need to have a sense of proportion about the things for which we are prepared to go out on a limb or even 'lay down our lives', so to speak. Too often we may have big convictions about little things and little convictions about big things. We may fuss about small issues and fail to recognise or be ready for the big challenges when they come. Again, a sense of proportion is important.

Sometimes we can be too close to a picture to be able to see it properly. We may become obsessed with the faults of our firm or our family and lose sight of the bigger picture with its sunshine as well as its shadows. Standing back may be an exercise well worth taking.

Talking with a good friend may help. He or she may not be able to tell us anything we don't already know, but through sharing we may be better able to get the facts into focus and deal with them appropriately. Taking a pen and paper and writing down the pros and cons of a case may also help us to sort things out and keep matters in proportion. Sometimes we allow problems to go round and round in our minds like garments in a tumble drier when they really need to be ironed out with firm common sense.

A Sense of Humour Helps

Winners have found various ways and means of keeping a sense of proportion and balance, even in times of difficulty. A sense of humour may help a lot. At times we may have taken ourselves too seriously. It has been said that very few people 'get their heads turned'—or become conceited—through trying to see the funny side of themselves!

As an antidote to pomposity a good prescription may be telling stories against oneself. Most of us have made many bloopers in our time and being willing to share some of them could be no bad thing.

For example, I recall that as a very young man I was working in a small mining town in Wales. I needed to arrange a display for which a wax model of a woman was required. A store in town agreed that I could borrow one and that I could pick it up on the

Saturday morning. No transport was available because for one thing, it was just after the war and petrol rationing was still in force in Britain.

Nothing daunted and somewhat unthinking, I presented myself at the store to make the collection. The model was taken out of the shop window and stripped of its clothes. Then, with a red face, I had to carry it through the crowded main street—followed by what, to my ears, sounded like gales of laughter. There was no way in which pomposity could survive that, but I made sure that when the model had to be returned it was so well wrapped that it could easily have passed as a roll of carpet!

Life may be a serious business but sometimes a little light relief will help us to get it into better focus. Strange as it sounds, it may sometimes make sense to give a little time to some light-hearted nonsense. We may have to be a little bit cracked before the light can get in!

Apart from humour there are other things which may help. During the great industrial depression the British Prime Minister, Stanley Baldwin, was in conference with a colleague. Things could hardly have been tougher. Suddenly Baldwin pointed to a beautiful vase of roses on the table and said, *'Bury your head in loveliness and thank God!'* Was that escapism or was it a recognition that beauty is more enduring than the troubles of the passing hour?

There is an old proverb which says:

> *'The bow that is always bent will soon cease to shoot straight'.*

That means that if we are too busy ever to relax we are probably too busy.

Field Marshall Earl Wavell, who was the British Commander-in-Chief in the Middle East during the second world war, found inspiration in the great poets when things were tough. Others have found music to be a means of keeping a sense of balance and proportion. Some have even found that an hour or so of fishing has been helpful.

Personally, I find it good to read some of the timeless passages in the Bible first thing in the morning. I write down my meditations and reflections in a special diary and that helps me to sort out the day and how I should cope with events, expected and unexpected. Of course, other people will have other ways.

Proportion and Priority

Keeping a sense of proportion will help us set our priorities. Stephen Covey in *First Things First* told of an instructor at a seminar who put a large jar next to a plate with some stones on it. He asked how many of the fist-sized stones could be put in the jar. After a few guesses he pushed in as many as he could and everyone agreed that the receptacle was full.

Then the lecturer reached under the table for a bucket from which he poured some gravel into the jar. He shook it so that the gravel went into the spaces between the stones. With a grin he asked if the jar was full now. Not to be caught twice the students replied that it was probably not.

He reached for another bucket from which he poured sand which went into the crevasses between the stones and the gravel. 'Full?' he asked. 'No', was the roared reply. Then he took a jug of water and poured close on a litre into the jar. 'So what's the point?' he asked. Somebody replied, 'If you really work at it you can always fit more into your life'.

'No!' the instructor said, 'The point I am making is—if you hadn't put those big rocks in first would you ever have got all of them in?'

Winners with a sense of proportion know the importance of putting first things first—so that they are not crowded out by trivia or at least by things of secondary importance.

Chapter Three

At Your Service

TIME was when petrol outlets were called 'service stations' and department stores had regiments of assistants waiting to serve the customers. Now 'self-service' is often the order of the day. But still, in the broad sense of the term, virtually all businesses exist to provide a service. If they do not meet a need there will soon be no reason for them to exist.

The same could be said of governments. Our political lords and masters need to reflect on the fact that their departments are often described as 'ministries'. They exist to serve the people and not the other way around.

When I was a boy in Wales it was customary to refer to a wealthy or influential man as 'big'. So, for example, Dai Jones might be 'a big man in the coal industry'. Perhaps we need to evaluate people as 'big' not according to what they have gathered to themselves in power or wealth, but rather by what they have been able to do for other people.

It may seem to stand current notions on their heads, but real winners are servants. Now some who have given marvellous service to the community have also prospered themselves.

It is interesting to hear about businesses that, during recession years, have done well, thank you very much! After twenty years in an Australian government department Robert decided to launch his own computer consultancy which in ten years has become a multi-million dollar business not only operating in Australia but in several other countries as well.

At first, Robert employed some high pressure sales persons but found that didn't work very well. Better results came not from fast-talking sales types or even from technical whizz-kids but from those who could relate to people and see problems from the client's point of view and then help them to find the answers Paradoxically, when the emphasis was on serving the client's interests the interests of the firm were best served—as the rapid and sustained growth of the business would testify.

Then let me tell you about Tom. He is an Australian and he is also a millionaire—although, to look at him sometimes in his very casual attire you might not think that he had two cents to rub together. When they were first married he and his wife Alice were not financially well off, their income depending upon Tom being able to hawk honey and home-made buns from door to door. They may have been relatively poor but they were happy and ready to work hard to eke out a living. At the same time they gave zealous voluntary service in the community.

One thing led to another and eventually Tom got into the building industry and struck it rich. Material goals were achieved but that didn't spoil Tom and Alice. They remained down to earth and ready to commit not only their money but their time and effort to helping those less fortunate than themselves. Tom used to say that if he had not been able to make money he would not have been able to help people in the way that he did.

When of retirement age, he and Alice journeyed to Melbourne to help a group of volunteers—including a number of homeless youths—refurbish a community centre. Tom rolled up his sleeves and worked with the lads, happy to give service and incidentally, provide a marvellous role model for the youngsters. Obviously, Tom had aimed to make money but the real goal of his life was (and is) to give service. In my book he is a winner.

For many years I was associated with the Rotary movement in various parts of the world. It was started by a man called Paul Harris to some extent on the basis of mutual self-interest. Men met and sought to further each other's business interests. Fortunately, the vision was extended and the needs of others were taken into account. 'Service above self' became and remains the main motto of the Rotary movement, another being, 'He profits most who serves best'. The idea is that Rotarians should genuinely seek to give good service to others through their vocations or business interests and also give service to the local and international communities on a voluntary basis.

Of course, the ideal of service was also implicit in the socialist dictum:

> 'To each according to his need, from each according to his ability'.

Unfortunately, human depravity has tended to subvert the ideal so that all too often it has become:

> 'To each according to his wants and from each as little as possible'

This has to be a recipe for disaster. But the ideal remains.

There is a Brighter Side

Part of the malaise afflicting our society lies in the fact that all too often we have become obsessed with our rights and oblivious to our responsibilities. Yet there is a brighter side to the human picture.

Peter Drucker, guru of management experts, has drawn attention to what is America's largest 'employer' although neither its workforce nor its output show up in the statistics. He says that one out of two adult Americans—a total of 90 million people—are estimated to work as volunteers, most of them in addition to holding down a paid job. If they were paid, their wages would amount to $150 billion a year.

While travelling around Australia I have been impressed by the vast amount of voluntary service given in this country also. Illustrations could be multiplied and many of them would feature young people. I have been talking to some very bright, up-and-coming young Australians imbued with the desire to serve. They are consciously choosing their professions with that goal in mind. Some will make a lot of money but that is not their main aim, surprising as some people may find that to be. There are those among them who are going to third world countries to work for a pittance. They are deliberately turning their backs on the prospect of big bank balances but who would dare to call them losers on that account?

The day before writing this I met a group of young people concerned about challenges nearer home such as the problems of homeless youth and drug use in schools. They have also started visiting young accident victims liable to spend long periods in Melbourne hospitals having fallen off their motor bikes or been injured in some other way. In addition to pursuing their studies or their jobs my young friends are ready to read or chat or play games with the patients who might otherwise be bored out of their young minds. No headlines are sought or found for that kind of youth activity, and yet at a time when we hear so much about mugging and drugging it makes a pleasant change.

Former President Harry Truman of the United States said words which are as true today as when he spoke them:

> *'The time is ripe not for an appeal to self-interest but to the hunger for great living which lies deep in the heart of every man. What young people need is not the chance of getting something for nothing but the opportunity of giving everything for something great'.*

Fortunately there are young people—and some older ones as well —who have latched on to this idea. In their jobs or professions or through voluntary service at home or abroad they are possessed with a desire to give service. They are 'servant leaders' and they are *real* winners.

Chapter Four

Courtesy Counts

COURTESY may not cost much but it can be worth a lot. Edward Wilson was on the ill-fated expedition to the South Pole with Captain Robert Scott in which both perished. He recorded that the thing which enabled the explorers to live together in small tents under terrible conditions without getting on each others' nerves was the fact that they never forgot to say 'please' and 'thank you'.

Courtesy counts in a family, an office, a club or wherever. It certainly pays in business. In the company hierarchy the telephonist may not rate highly but he or she may sometimes be as influential in securing (or losing!) customers as the managing director. If an initial phone enquiry is treated in an off-hand manner the prospect of an order may be killed, stone dead, whereas a warm and courteous response could be the beginning of a deal. Of course, it may sometimes be necessary to keep a caller waiting but never without apology or explanation. When, as a senior executive I used to telephone my office, I was sometimes glad when my voice was not recognised as I could then gauge how other callers might be treated. I knew that the whole organisation might be judged by the response of one employee on the end of a telephone line.

At a manufacturing firm in Melbourne, the receptionist has a notice on her desk which describes her role: 'Director of first impressions'. Obviously, someone realises the importance of her task.

It should go without saying that courtesy in letters is a must. It may be necessary to make a point forcibly but rudeness is invariably counter-productive. On a couple of occasions I have seen letters so fiery that they would have been better written on asbestos—or better still, not written at all. Such letters may not only wound recipients, they may rise up and haunt their authors.

A man once confided in me and spoke of a desire to see his personal file held by the organisation for which he worked. I told him that in his country that was legally his right and then, knowing him well and being aware of his tendency to write first and think later, I gently suggested that perhaps the most distressing documents he would find on file might be the letters he had written himself. He must have taken the point for, as far as I know, he never asked to see his file!

Thanks a lot

The courtesy of a 'thank you' never goes amiss. If we're too busy to acknowledge services rendered or work well done—we're too busy. In our homes and in our places of employment most of us rely heavily on the efforts of others and expressing appreciation can help to enhance the spirit of co-operation. (If possible we should praise publicly but almost always reprimand privately.)

I recall a day when, feeling rather pleased with myself, I remarked, 'I have written more than fifty letters today'. My faithful secretary looked at me with what I thought was admiration in her eyes and then she said, very demurely, 'It's wonderful what one man can accomplish—when he doesn't have to do the work himself!' I laughed, conceded the point and expressed my appreciation—not for the first time, I may say.

Some people are almost dying for want of the oxygen of appreciation. In their work they do their best and are lucky if they get as much as a grunt of acknowledgment. Before retirement, in my own leadership role, I tried to express personal thanks to as many people working under my direction as possible. However, latterly, with more than 12,000 staff spread over a large country there were limits to what I could do on a person-to-person basis. It became necessary to encourage others to show appreciation.

However, I did send out a letter of appreciation to all employees once a year and while I didn't expect thanks for my thanks I hoped that my sincere appreciation was appreciated, nonetheless!

If it is true that people may feel unappreciated in the workaday world then it is also true in the family circle where we may all tend to take a lot for granted. Could that be a cause of marital breakdowns and family breakups?

Lack of appreciation produces a lose-lose situation—and yet the remedy is in the hands of all of us. The words 'think' and 'thank' are related. Certainly, if we think we will have cause to thank—and be more likely to be winners as a result.

If we are running a business, we are unlikely to win all the orders we might seek but expressing thanks for being considered may leave the door open for further opportunities in the future. Taking the trouble to express thanks when prompt deliveries are made will help to cement a business relationship and augur well for future service.

I once did a stint as the editor of a weekly paper and made a point of acknowledging all the articles and poems sent in—even if they were quite unsuitable for publication. Apart from this being a courtesy due to people who had spent time and effort and money on postage, it kept the door open for a few whose second efforts were much more promising. In any case, I felt that a thank you was never wasted.

Promises, Promises

My grandmother had a rather quaint saying. She would often remark, 'Some people's promises are like pie-crusts, made to be broken.' She was right. I have learnt that the value of a promise depends upon the character of the person who makes it and I believe that real winners take and make promises seriously.

Representatives of firms sometimes promise to ring back with information or send a written quotation and then fail to do so and make no apology. This may be due to poor communication within the firm or mean that members of staff do not cope or care. Whatever the reason, it is bad for business.

Then in all too many cases delivery dates are not met, again with no apology or explanation being offered. Some of the firms concerned spend huge sums of money on advertising and even have public relations experts on staff. But broken promises are bad public relations. The customer who has stayed at home all day waiting for a delivery or at least a phoned explanation of the reason for delay is unlikely to be impressed by advertising hype in the media.

Like honesty, courtesy is the best policy, mainly because it is evidence of the concern for the other person which is the mark of the real winner.

Hilaire Belloc wrote:

> *Of courtesy it is much less*
> *Than courage of heart or holiness,*
> *Yet in my walks it seems to me*
> *That the Grace of God is in courtesy.*

Chapter Five

'People People'

IN MOST FIELDS winners need to be 'people people'. That is, they need to work *with* and *through* and *for* other folk, which is not always easy. Some people are like centipedes with corns on every foot; you can't get near them without stepping on their corns! Mind, it is just possible that others may find us a bit difficult on occasion!

Be that as it may, without the ability to get along with people many other talents may be of little value. If we are in the commercial field enlightened self-interest should tell us that it is essential to relate to people. Our livelihood depends upon it. But nice guys want to relate to people for their own sake.

Coming back to live in Australia after a number of years, I am pleased at the way in which in government departments and at least some stores, there is an obvious attempt to be 'people sensitive' and provide personal attention. That helps to make doing business a pleasure and is one of the things which marks this country out as special. Friendliness and helpfulness cost little but mean a lot.

Despite this, here as elsewhere, there are subtle ways in which people may feel depersonalised, unless we are careful.

In another country, I heard of a canvasser going from door to door gathering information about residents. 'How many live in these premises?' he asked one woman. 'Well,' she replied, 'there's Billy and Mary and Megan and...' Curtly, the canvasser cut in, 'I'm not interested in names, only numbers', he said.

I talked to Pat, a 'people person' if ever there was one. She is a vivacious and dynamic mother of three, now retired. After gaining suitable qualifications she entered the hotel industry at a time when there was considerable resistance to women in executive positions. In due course she proved that women could be dignified, authoritative and effective and was able to hold down positions of increasing influence.

Her particular concern was to ensure that staff as well as patrons were treated properly and her point of view as a woman helped in this. I think that she would agree that managers have no more right to be careless with human resources than surgeons. Pat is not a 'preachy' type but her own confidence and faith led some to see her as a friend as well as a manager. On leaving the hotel industry she went into local government and, as a councillor, worked indefatigably for the elderly and vulnerable in her area.

There is always a danger that we may *love things* and *use people* instead of at least trying to love people and use things. To some extent it may be inevitable that we tend to see folk as stereotypes —customers, patients, clients employees or whatever—and may almost lose sight of the fact that they are people, unless we are careful. It may be said that some professionals have to remain somewhat detached from those they seek to help in order to cope. That is understandable, but unless we are careful we can become too adept at the impersonal approach to fellow human beings.

G.K. Chesterton wrote a marvellous essay about the English jury system. He said that for judges and lawyers who spent half their lives in courts there was always the danger that they would simply see the usual 'prisoner at the bar' whereas twelve ordinary citizens chosen at random would be more likely to see the human being in the dock as a person like themselves, to be judged accordingly.

Legislation alone may not entirely change attitudes but it can help. In many countries anti-discrimination laws have made people aware that there are right and wrong ways of treating others—particularly those who may be vulnerable in some way.

People do have a right to do their work and pursue their leisure activities without harassment on account of their gender, colour, race or whatever. Therefore the hallmark of respect should be on all our dealings.

Two Ears and One Mouth

We were given two ears and one mouth but some of us are very slow to take the hint! However, we would be much better 'people people' if we were more ready to listen to others. We may be well-meaning at times but too eager to foist our solutions on to folk instead of giving them a chance to share their perceptions.

I have heard of employers who, with all good intentions have, for example, provided gym or child-care facilities for employees without doing sufficient research among those for whom the provision was intended. As a result the provision has not been tailored to needs and may have been little used.

I guess that I have sometimes been no better than others in this respect, but I have made a point of meeting many groups of people, for whom I have had a measure of responsibility, and giving them opportunity to raise points or ask questions. I'm not sure how much they may have learnt from my answers at times, but I have certainly learnt a lot from their questions, and that has been to my benefit.

Whatever our position or role may be we can always gain through trying to step into other people's shoes and through trying to see things from their perspective. I remember spending time with an admirable woman who was of very tiny stature. Rather uncharacteristically, she opened up and shared her frustration at not being able to reach books on the library shelves and having to jostle with people who seemed to tower above her in the queue. It was good to see things from her point of view, even to a limited extent.

I have talked to others who have been confined to wheelchairs and who have spoken about 'unfriendly buildings'—that is, buildings difficult to access. Such conversations have made me anxious, before approving plans for new buildings, to ensure that we went even beyond the requirements of the planning authorities if necessary in order to make the facilities 'friendly' and inviting.

Because of modern means of travel and communication the world seems to be shrinking all the time. It is becoming a neighbourhood which makes it important that we try to be neighbourly. In first world countries many people eat themselves to death. We might say that they dig their graves with their knives and forks! At the same time, to travel in Africa or South America for example, as I have done, is to see poverty and hunger that can cause nightmares. It has been said that if everyone *cared* enough and everyone *shared* enough everyone would *have* enough. That's a big 'if' but the alternatives are too terrible to contemplate.

As a result of the economic recession some countries have cut back on overseas aid. Hopefully, this will only be a temporary measure. I sat in a committee when it was announced that because of 'cut-backs' it would no longer be possible to send large consignments of milk powder to certain needy areas. A fellow member of the committee who had lived and worked in the places in question was near to tears as he explained that we were literally cutting off the lifeline which kept many children alive. That helped us to see beyond economic figures to human facts, beyond the paper to the people. We all need to do that if we are to play even a little part in winning a better world.

"We were given two ears and one mouth but some of us are very slow to take the hint."

Chapter Six

Confidence in Confidence?

IT IS SAID that in a battle between the imagination and the will the imagination is likely to come off best. Let me illustrate that. If a plank of wood was placed on the ground most of us could probably walk along it without any difficulty. We would imagine ourselves doing it easily and it would therefore be unlikely to present any problem.

But what if that same piece of wood was placed between two high-rise buildings? The thought of walking along the plank might then be enough to scare us stiff. We would picture ourselves losing our balance and falling and although we might summon up our courage, nervousness could well cause us to fall and fulfil our worst fears. In a contest between will and imagination the latter may well triumph. But why should they be in conflict anyway? Couldn't they support each other and work together?

Now, we are unlikely to be into walking planks anyway, but there is a principle here which may also apply to many other things we might want to do. When by an exercise of will we resolve to do a task we should imagine ourselves succeeding and thereby greatly increase the likelihood of that happening.

Instead of summoning up our courage and saying 'I *will* be successful' we should relax and say 'I *can* do this thing' and picture ourselves doing so. We should reverse the words, 'Can I?' and say, 'I can!' Then, all things being equal, we will be winners.

Henry Ford said:

> *'If you believe you can do a thing or if you believe you cannot—you are right'.*

'If you believe you can do a thing or if you believe you cannot—you are right'. — **Henry Ford**

Having Confidence Well Based

In the musical *The Sound of Music* there is a song which speaks of 'having confidence in confidence' which is fair enough, as far as it goes. But in the real world confidence needs some support and I would mention three things which, like the legs of a stool, may provide this.

First, there is competence. Sometimes competence without confidence may not be sufficient, but confidence without competence could be disastrous. Just imagine putting yourself in the hands of a character who fancied himself as a surgeon and wielded a scalpel with great confidence but without adequate training or proven ability! From such a guy we would run a mile! If people are to have confidence and inspire it in others then obviously they need to know their stuff. They need to be masters of their craft, truly professional, apart from anything else. I know a doctor like that.

Ian speaks confidently about the AIDS problem. He is an expert with an international reputation. He knows that he knows because he has studied the virus in many countries. And when on occasion I have spoken to him on the subject, perhaps with particular cases in mind, I have drawn on his confidence and have been glad that, in addition to being very able, he is also deeply caring—a nice guy and a real winner, in fact.

If we want to feel confident then for one thing we had better make sure that in our chosen field we have taken the trouble to make sure that we really know what we are talking about.

Then, confidence may be based on experience. We may sometimes reflect on the advantages of being young but one of the advantages of getting older is that often, when faced with difficulties, it is possible to recall similar problems in the past and how we were able to solve them. Experience may be dearly bought but it is invaluable.

If sometimes we feel that we do not have much personal experience we can probably talk with others who have been there and done that before us. It is great when fine people who have been winners in their particular field are ready to share their hard-won experience with others. They are confidence-builders and worth their weight in gold. In fact, one way of being a winner is to help others to win and pass on some of our knowledge and experience to those who will follow.

Confidence may also be based on faith. St Paul once said, 'I can do everything...' He wasn't being 'big headed' or anything like that. Far from it! As the context of his remark makes plain, he was referring to the tremendous boost of confidence which he found through his personal faith.

Winners must maintain confidence in themselves and in what they are doing. That may not always be easy. Self-doubt attacks us all at times. We question what we are on about and wonder whether it is worthwhile. We wonder whether we can really make a difference—or if anyone can make a difference in our kind of situation. The short answer is that we can, and we should!

Chapter Seven

Support Systems Can Help

PROPER support makes a difference in many fields of activity. For example, a football team can be buoyed and inspired by loyal supporters. In a military operation those actually fighting must depend heavily on those providing support.

It is the same in many professions. For example, those involved in counselling will probably feel the need for supervision and support. Many others may look for mentors—people with the experience and wisdom to advise or, at least, act as sounding boards.

Far from being a sign of weakness it may be an indication of wisdom when people arrange support systems for themselves. Of course, there are some folk who are naturally 'leaners' and others who seem to be born leaders, but even the strongest will probably need support and should arrange for this.

Those who best support us may not be those who nearly always agree with us. Rather, they will be those who will tell us what we need to hear rather than just what we want to hear. Real winners don't feel the need to surround themselves with 'yes-people' but rather prefer those who will lift performance by constructive criticism seasoned with necessary encouragement.

With many key positions support staff will necessarily go with the job. Winners are wise enough to support their supporters and give them scope to be as helpful as they can be. I knew an executive who wanted to give an impression of omni-competence — not that anyone was taken in! He seemed to feel that it was a disgrace to admit that he didn't know everything. Supporters and advisers were kept at a distance. In any case, what was the good of trying to advise someone who knew it all anyway?

Winners are Wiser

Without ceasing to be their own men or women, capable of making proper judgements, winners prefer their decisions to rest on a broad base of experience and knowledge rather than on their unsupported hunches.

Many people find tremendous support in their families. It is not literally true that behind every good man there is a good woman, any more than it is true that behind every good woman there is a good man. Nevertheless, many who have achieved great things owe much to the solid support of a spouse.

Bringing up Parents

Children can sometimes do a tremendous job in bringing up their parents! How they pounce on a corny gag or an out-moded idea! Sometimes they have to be reminded that wisdom was not born with their generation, but for all that they can be an invaluable support.

Anyone has a head start if supported by a loyal family. It has been said that many a saint's reputation depends upon the silence of his or her family, and there may be something in that even for those who wouldn't reckon themselves to be saints. Of course, family loyalty and support cannot be taken for granted; it may need to be earned and is not always forthcoming, even then.

But to be able to win at home and build strong domestic support there is a worthy aim. More is the pity that, with increased mobility, the extended family now often tends to be fragmented, and sometimes the lines of communication are broken and in need of repair. Time spent on attempting to effect such repairs can never be wasted.

Friendships

Apart from the support of a family there is much to be said for the support of friends. Harry Emerson Fosdick said that a person's bare individuality was like the bit of grit that got into the oyster shell. The pearl of his or her life was made by the relationships they gathered around them.

True friendship is a gift of incalculable value. It can scarcely be bought. In fact, friends who have to be bought are unlikely to be worth what is paid for them. But if a true friendship comes into our life then we should nurture and not neglect it.

Winston Churchill said of his war-time colleague Lord Beaverbrook, *'Max is a foul weather friend'*. Again, referring to Beaverbrook (then Minister of Aircraft Production) in the British House of Commons on 22nd January, 1941, Churchill declared, *'He is at his very best when things are at their very worst'*.

In *Great Expectations* Charles Dickens told how Pip went to visit for the last time his benefactor, Magwitch, the dying ex-convict who had been condemned to be hanged. The convict took Pip's hand and said:

> *'You've never deserted me, dear boy, and what's best of all, you've been more comfortable alonger me since I was under a dark cloud than when the sun shone. That's best of all'*.

Another famous English writer, George Eliot wrote:

> *"Oh the comfort, the inexpressible comfort of feeling safe with a person, having neither to weigh thoughts nor measure words, but pour them all out, just as they are chaff and grain together... (knowing that) a faithful hand will take and sift them, keep what is worth keeping and with a breath of kindness blow the rest away.'*

People with friends like that are rich and can only be strengthened.

I have mentioned the support of colleagues, family and friends. I would also refer to the support of a worthy faith or philosophy. This is not an overtly religious book. It is my hope that many of the principles I have shared will find acceptance with people of various religions and of no religion. However, I must say that personally I have found great support in my Christian faith. Nothing—but nothing—has been more important.

" Many people find tremendous support in their families."

It was not a preacher man but the late King George VI who, in one of his Christmas broadcasts from war-time Britain, quoted the following lines:

I said to the man who stood at the gate of the year 'Give me a light that I may tread safely into the unknown'.

And He replied:

'Go out into the darkness and put your hand into the hand of God. That shall be to you better than a light and safer than a known way.

Chapter Eight

Facing Failure

MOTIVATIONAL books are often replete with success stories but say little about the failure which sometimes attends the best efforts. Someone quipped, 'If at first you don't succeed you're running about normal!' But what if you don't succeed after repeated efforts? Does it mean that you're a born loser? Not at all, but it may certainly feel like it.

After addressing a meeting I said 'Hi!' to a teenage lad in the audience who I had never met before. All he could blurt out was, 'I've tried for seventy jobs'—and I was sad as I looked into eyes dulled by a sense of rejection.

I know a very able man in his twenties—a doctor of philosophy —who, when his university contract ran out found himself unemployed for months and applied for a hundred jobs before securing a position. He was resilient in spirit but repeated knock backs were hard to take, for all that.

Now of course, losing jobs in a recession may not represent any failure on the part of the persons concerned but may be due to economic or political factors quite outside their control. Yet they may well feel a sense of failure mixed with anger, resentment and despair. And that has to be faced.

If generous retrenchment packages are available it is helpful and at least it makes the economic prospects brighter. It may even make job-loss appear as a blessing in disguise. But this is not necessarily so. At the height of the recession I was approached by the president of the service club to which I belonged. He said, 'Wesley, I am wondering if some kind of counselling should be provided for eight guys in the club who have lost their jobs recently. They are really hurting'. Some of those men had been very high-fliers in the corporate sector. They were unlikely to be without a few dollars behind them, but they were smarting at the fact that they were no longer wanted by institutions to which, in some cases, they had given all their working lives.

During recent years thousands of businesses have gone to the wall. That has not only meant serious financial losses for some but also a devastating sense of personal diminution and loss of self-worth. But it is important to remember that it's not what life does *to* us but what it does *in* us that matters most. In other words, what counts is how we respond to events.

Some people face failure in the academic field. Recently, I talked with a self-made multi-millionaire who confessed that he had always struggled academically. After leaving school at 15 he took 17 years to get a degree in commerce and wondered whether that was a record. He had difficulty in persuading university authorities to allow him to continue with his studies, but he doggedly refused to accept defeat and finally won through.

Making a Success of Failure

Of course, there may be times when our difficulties are of our own making, when, as Shakespeare put it, the fault is *'not in our stars'* but in ourselves. We may have blown it in some way and find it difficult to forgive ourselves. The question then is, where do we go from here?

We may have failed (who hasn't?) but we need not be losers.

Sometimes failure can be turned to good account. For example, having failed a job interview it may be an idea to phone the firm, thank them for giving consideration to the application and ask if they could give any idea as to why it had not been accepted. Such information, if given, might help future submissions—even to the same firm.

Sometimes an error can be turned into a service opportunity by someone who shows concern for any inconvenience caused to the other party. The aim should be never to waste a failure but rather turn it into some kind of gain.

I know a man who was made redundant by the firm for which he had worked since leaving school more than thirty years before. It was a shock to his system and seemed an unmitigated disaster. In fact, it turned out to be a blessing in disguise because it made him explore new avenues. In the end, he was actually better off financially.

None of us can go back; we can only go forward. We can't relive the past, but we can outlive it. As it has been said, we need to accept what can't be changed, change what should be changed —and have the wisdom to know the difference.

So far as I am concerned, that will take vital faith—which might be defined as 'an invisible means of support'. It will also take courage and 'possibility thinking'. There's life after failure but we shouldn't wallow in our misery; we need to get up and get going.

Thomas Carlyle was poor and needed cash from the publication of his work on the French Revolution, the fruit of years of effort. Perhaps on the understanding that every writer needs an editor and an honest critic, Carlyle asked his friend John Stuart Mill to read it. Unfortunately, a servant-girl in Mill's house inadvertently used the manuscript to light a fire. Enough to shatter a man? You would think so. In fact, Carlyle rewrote the whole thing from start to finish and achieved fame and fortune as a result.

Success and failure may be relative terms and sometimes the difference between the one and the other may be marginal. Not always does the best man or woman win in an obvious way, but in another sense those who continue to come back fighting are always winners within themselves, where victory is most important.

Getting a Jump Start

Sometimes a good friend can help to give us the 'jump start' we need.

Some years ago I was by Temple Gardens near the Thames Embankment in London, England, in the early hours of a wintry morning, and felt concerned about people who were sleeping in cardboard packing cases or on park benches.

Suddenly, a smartly dressed 'city gent' got out of an expensive car and came and spoke to me. 'A little while ago I was sleeping on one of these benches', he said. I was astonished. Then he explained that he had been wrongly accused of impropriety and struck off his professional register.

This had so upset him that he had 'let himself go' until in deep depression he was sleeping out on park benches. One night a man he did not know but who seemed to know something about him said, 'Why don't you try and get your old job back? I'll do some casual work in the market and get you some money to get decent clothes'.

Incredibly, a few nights later the stranger handed over the money and the shock of grateful surprise jolted the dispirited man into action. To cut a long story short, he had appealed against his deregistration and had been reinstated in employment.

Months later he had been out looking for the guy to whom he owed so much, with the thought that he might in turn set him up in accommodation and possible employment. That night he had found his man and was so thrilled to tell me the astonishing story.

Granted that the case is somewhat extreme, it illustrates that although people may be down they need never be out. They may feel that they are on the scrap heap but they can be recycled, for failure need not be final.

Chapter Nine

Take Courage

FEW WOULD doubt that it takes courage to be a winner. Bravery is not difficult to recognise and it is easy to admire. We appreciate the courage of the long-distance runner or the executive ready to do what is right and take the tough decisions when necessary. We marvel at the way in which some folk face up to sickness or tragedy of some kind and feel sure that we could never cope in such circumstances. But who knows?

I recall a very special parade which took place in London, England. Those who took part were holders of the Victoria Cross. There was no spit or polish and little if any of the panache associated with some processions. One onlooker said to another, 'They look a very ordinary lot'. His companion replied, 'Yes, but ordinary people are capable of very great valour!'

True enough, but how do we define valour or courage?

Some might say that courage is the absence of fear—but is that right? I don't think so. An absence of fear may be not so much evidence of bravery as of foolhardiness. Imagine a person with no fear of fire or falling or danger of any kind! Such a person wouldn't be a hero or a heroine, he or she would be mentally deficient!

Sometimes the absence of fear is not so much evidence of courage as proof of ignorance. Some of us might move about parts of an atomic plant without a trace of fear. No thought of danger might enter our heads whereas a nuclear scientist in a similar situation might blanch with fear. Would that mean that we were heroic and he was a coward? Not at all. It would simply mean that we were ignorant of the dangers and he was not.

Of course, there are fears which are irrational and phobias which may be more common than we suspect. Special help may be needed to deal with these, but there are natural fears common to most people. If we are fearful at times, it is quite normal. Fear is not necessarily something to fear.

In one fine poem, Ethel Alder has the line:

'Courage is fear that has said its prayers'.

In other words, courage is not the absence of fear but its conquest.

Such a Coward

Mary Mowatt was the long-time matron of St Peter's Hospital, Stepney, in the east end of London. During the second world war when air raids ravaged that part of the city there were patients on the top floor of the hospital. When the guns boomed and the bombs fell their distress was terrible to see. Then, in would come the matron, composed and calm, moving from bed to bed, taking the terror from the patients. Her courage was a byword. She was a winner, for sure.

After the war Mary Mowatt surprised some of her former patients by saying, 'I was such a coward. When the raids began my whole system seemed to collapse. I just stood up and said, 'O God... I am terrified, but you can save my poor patients in the top floor wards. Help them... I cannot!' That was her way of controlling her own fear and instilling confidence in others.

Other people will have different ways of finding the courage to be and do what life demands. In his book, *Profiles of Courage* John F. Kennedy quoted Ernest Hemmingway's definition of courage as 'grace under pressure'. Sometimes the pressure is sudden—like the need to risk one's life in order to save a drowning child or rescue someone from a burning building. People who match such demands with an heroic response are rightly regarded as winners, but sometimes there is a call for courage over a long haul.

John Buchan in his book, *Mr Standfast,* records the following words of Peter Pienar:

> *'The big courage is the cold-blooded kind, that never lets go even when you are feeling empty inside, and your blood's thin, and there's no kind of fun or profit to be had, and the trouble's not over in an hour or two, but lasts for months and years. One of the men here was speaking about that kind, and he called it "fortitude". I reckon fortitude's the biggest thing a man can have — just to go on enduring when there's no heart or guts left in you...'*

Sometimes I have had to summon up courage to deal with a difficult situation when there has been the temptation to sweep matters under the carpet or leave them to someone else. Then there have been the times when decisions have had to be made with foresight—and the knowledge that they would be judged by people looking back with the advantage of hindsight—with which anyone can be as wise as Socrates!

I recall an occasion when I had some responsibility in connection with the building of a big centre for community and charitable work in the centre of a large city. It had been decided that valuable air space above the centre would be utilised through the building of a tower block of offices to produce ongoing rental income which, in turn, would support further charitable work.

At a critical stage the recession set in and there was a surplus of office accommodation in the area. Some advisers said that we should delete the tower block from the plans as otherwise it would remain empty for years, a 'white elephant' and a monument to our foolishness. Others felt that it was a case of 'now or never'.

Having weighed varying expert advice and sought guidance it was a matter of taking courage. As a matter of interest, my colleagues and I decided that the tower block should be built and within a reasonable time it was fully leased—but such a good result was not easy to predict at the time.

Those who aspire to leadership should know that at times it means going out on a limb. There must be cautious courage. All issues having been examined decisions should be taken in good faith. To be a winner it is necessary to run the risk of losing at times. If anyone is too timid to take that risk then winning is not for them.

Chapter Ten

Saving Time

WE HAVE more time-saving gadgets than ever before. But whatever happens to the time being saved? Thanks to medical science people are living longer—and yet, nearly everyone says that they're short of time. Interesting!

Of course, really wise guys make good use of whatever time they have for, after all, it is the raw material of life. Everyone alive has the same allocation each day—1,440 valuable minutes—but what people make of those minutes varies enormously. Some who wouldn't dream of deliberately taking their own lives allow them to drip or dribble away through wasting time.

I understand that beneath a clock in a Commonwealth Bank in Perth, Western Australia, there was placed a notice which read:

> *Lost*
>
> *Lost yesterday, somewhere between sunrise and sunset, two golden hours, each with sixty diamond minutes. No reward is offered for they are gone forever.*

Peter Drucker wrote:

'Time management takes perseverance and self-discipline, but no other investment pays higher dividends'.

Without doubt, the management of our time is both an art and a craft.

There may be value in conducting an audit of the way in which we spend our days. For a week we could record in a notebook just how we have spent time—a brief phrase entered every waking half-hour should be sufficient. For example, one entry might be, 'driving to work' another, 'taking a tea break' yet another, 'consulting over the XYZ project'. At the end of the week we could evaluate our allocation of time. Have we given enough 'quality time' to the family? How much was routine work affected by interruptions? Was some time wasted on non-essentials?

If undertaken conscientiously that kind of audit could help us in our time management. If we are less than honest in the exercise then who do we think we are fooling? Of course, we don't need to become obsessed with the passing of time. The clock and the calendar are not meant to be tyrants. But they cannot be ignored either.

Twenty Years Asleep

By the way, it is something to ponder that a person who lives to be seventy years of age is likely to have spent more than twenty years of life asleep and say, five or six years eating!

To be good stewards of our time we must plan our work (as well as our leisure)—that is assuming that we have some freedom to organise our time.

As a young fellow I had a chief who had a dictum which he quoted in season and out of season. My friends and I smiled at its repeated use but it was not lost on us, for all that. He used to say, *'Plan your work and work your plan'*. Failure to do that is a sure way to waste time. As is often said, 'To fail to plan is to plan to fail'.

In our planning we should be a little flexible. We must expect the unexpected and the untimely interruptions which affect most people. But at least, if we have set a course we will not be drifting aimlessly on a sea of circumstances and will be far more likely to reach the harbour of achievement.

"Time management takes perseverance and self-discipline" — **Peter Drucker**

Then it is important to prioritise our tasks, taking care to distinguish between the urgent and the important. It might be an idea to number the things which need to be done, always bearing in mind the constraints of the time available.

We need to be wise to ourselves. If for example we are prone to put off unpleasant tasks perhaps we should put them first on our list and get them over. Again, if we are 'morning people' perhaps the most demanding assignments should be tackled in the morning when we are at our best. If we are 'night people' then that may be taken into account.

We may come to the conclusion that some tasks shouldn't be on our list, anyway. Perhaps the right thing would be to say no to some requests, if that is possible. Now here I had better confess that I am not preaching what I have always practised. I have often found it difficult to refuse to do things when asked. But nice guys or not, we sometimes need to say no.

Careful consideration may indicate that some tasks do not justify time being spent on them. The fact that some things have always been done does not mean that they need to be done for ever and ever, amen. Sometimes our key word should be eliminate. There should be no need to waste time on useless activity when there are so many useful things waiting to be done.

Delegation not Abdication

As we preview the tasks needing attention we may find it necessary to delegate. Now, delegation is not the same as abdication. We may still have to carry ultimate responsibility but it may be right for someone else to do the 'leg work' and free us for other tasks. Some find it difficult to delegate. They may feel with some justification that others will not perform as well as they could, but in trying to do everything themselves they may end up like jugglers with too many balls in the air and almost certain to let some things fall.

When delegating it is important to choose the people we trust and trust the people we choose. There is hardly anything worse for a conscientious worker than to be crowded by his or her superior and not given space to do the task required. At the same time, experience teaches that, with some people, particularly, there is need to check. There are those who will do what you *inspect* rather than what you *expect*! Of course, in all cases it is important to make clear just what we do expect and when.

Paradoxically, if we are to fill our time usefully we will need to give ourselves (and our colleagues) breaks from time to time. The musician will be used to having rests indicated on the music sheet, and in other fields of activity breaks may be vital. They may be brief breaks to walk around the office or change physical position, or they may be something more. We all need the chance to catch our mental breath on occasion and far from being a waste of time this may be a very wise use of it. The word re-creation speaks for itself and makes clear the need to re-create depleted resources.

In addition to breaks some rewards may not be inappropriate. Some of us have tended to treat ourselves far worse than we would ever have treated people under our direction. Without being over-indulgent, we might allow ourselves the luxury of a meal out or an evening in on completion of a project. Anticipation of such a 'reward' may well keep our spirits from flagging before the day is half done. The desire to make the best use of our time should not turn us into workaholics. Time allocated for necessary rest may be well spent.

Work Smart

A very successful businessman surprised me by saying, 'It is not my wish that my people or I should work too hard or too long. What I want is that we should "work smart"'.

Among other things, 'working smart' will mean getting the desired results with economy of time and effort. The use of modern methods and technology will help. In an age of computerisation, for example, it doesn't make sense to work as if we were still in the era of the horse and buggy.

Then 'working smart' may mean being organised and getting our act together. It may mean 'working tidy'. When my friends and I were young fellows we would say, laughingly, that an untidy desk indicated a tidy mind. That was sheer rubbish. Of course, some people with very untidy desks (or work benches) do a very good job but that is in spite of untidyness not because of it. We may waste hours looking for lost files or other items. I know from experience! However, valuable time can be saved by remembering such mottoes as, 'A place for everything and everything in its place!' or 'Don't put it down, put it away!'

Rather than being cluttered with a mass of papers it is better to have on the desk only what requires immediate attention, other items being in 'bring up files' or wherever. Obviously, there will be some documents which have to be perused on several occasions but where possible it is good to aim at only handling papers once. Constant paper shuffling is time-consuming. The same kind of principle holds in other than office situations. We should aim to 'work smart'.

The way in which people use time may be an indication of their character. A conscientious employee will feel that to waste time for which he or she has been paid would be a form of theft. But many people will also feel an obligation to use quality time for their family or in helping those less fortunate, for example. Then we all owe it to ourselves to use time for self-improvement and legitimate leisure. Perhaps the trick is to get things in proper balance. As one writer put it a long time ago:

> *'Teach us to number our days aright, that we may gain a heart of wisdom'.*

Chapter Eleven

Managing to Lead

I HAVE in mind two men for whom I have considerable regard. I'll call the first James. He is a master of detail. One has only to sketch the broad outline of a project and then, with confidence, James can be left to work it out and bring matters to a successful conclusion. He is the kind of man any leader should cherish but he is not a natural leader himself. He is superb when working out a predetermined concept but put him in a leadership position and he is likely to falter. Left to work out his own game plan and dream up new ideas or policies he has difficulty.

I'll call my second example Tony. He is articulate in several languages, an inspiring talker and remarkably innovative and inventive. He is a pioneer who can inspire others to great endeavours and for that reason is worth his weight in gold. But, when it comes to correspondence and routine desk work he really must be one of the world's worst! And his failure to deal with routine matters can be costly.

These two men happen to work in different countries but they are types who need each other. Both play invaluable roles in their respective organisations but both need complementing. Management and leadership are necessary in any organisation. If the roles can be combined to some extent in the same people all well and good, otherwise it is essential to place personnel in such a way that balanced direction can be ensured.

Professor John P. Kotter has written:

'While improving...ability to lead, companies should
remember that strong leadership with weak management is

> *no better, and is sometimes actually worse, than the reverse.*
> *The real challenge is to combine strong leadership and*
> *strong management and use each to balance the other'.*

If we compare management and leadership it should not be to the detriment of one or the other; both are important. It might be said that a manager moves paper while a leader moves—or inspires—people. The one copes with complexity while the other embraces change.

The typical manager finds security in short and long range planning—which is not a bad thing. However, the leader may be more flexible and ready to set a new direction in a changing situation.

Warren Bennis and Burt Nannas in their book, *Leaders* produced the aphorism:

> *'Managers do things right. Leaders do the right things'.*

Of course, like most one-liners it is an over-simplification, but it makes a worthwhile point for all that. We might add that leaders are intent on making things happen while others may be only concerned with what is happening.

Over-Managed and Under-Led

It is claimed that many companies and organisations are over-managed and under-led and that may be true. So what is the answer? It will not be found through beating the breast and bemoaning the absence of those giants said to have walked the earth in the dream-time when companies were young and the world was green.

Granted that some people may be 'born' managers or leaders— or even born manager/leaders—the fact is that generally, the kind of people we need will have to be fashioned through training and exposure to make or break experiences. I have found that 'team leadership' at middle management level helps to prepare some people for more senior responsibilities. Perhaps the greatest need is to spot potential early and develop it fully—notwithstanding the difficulties faced in an increasingly mobile society.

There may be value in sharing prospects for future promotion with promising employees in order to retain their loyalty. The only danger in that is that through unforeseen circumstances there may turn out to be more candidates for promotion than vacancies. Then some of those concerned may feel that they have been sold short and that the only way up is the way out. Long-range planning for personnel is important but sometimes even the best laid plans can be thrown into disarray by unexpected developments.

Those who would be 'nice guys' and 'winners' in the field of management and leadership will need a whole range of qualities and abilities. Many of them are indicated elsewhere in this book. Here I would highlight a few which I believe to be of particular importance.

Qualities and Abilities

First, I would mention vision. I have in mind the ability to see beyond things as they are to things as they could be. Sometimes visions may be mystical experiences but more often they arise out of a down-to-earth examination of a situation and a very practical assessment of how it might be improved. To be effective a vision must be translated into an appropriate strategy and be given practical expression. Visionary leadership must be supported by managerial efficiency.

Sometimes a vision for the future may be laced with innovative ideas. At other times it may feature some very old ideas patterned or applied in new ways. Because an insight is not original does not mean that it may not be valuable. Sometimes we have to go back to go forward! We may need to recapture the vision which inspired those who went before us.

A vision of how a company could be more effective might come to a very junior partner or employee. No matter! What counts is not who has the inspired vision but who is prepared to go with it. A true leader will recognise value in a vision even when it is not his own. As a flash of lightning can illuminate a landscape so the shared vision of a company or community renewed can give a new sense of purpose and direction.

A vision without a task is a dream,

A task without a vision is drudgery,

A vision with a task is the hope of the world.

Then the effective manager/leader will need to be a person of hope. Abraham Lincoln said, *'An essential quality of leadership is a large hopefulness'.* Winners are not daunted by difficulty or put off by problems.

At 10 Downing Street, London, his prime-ministerial home during the war, Winston Churchill put up a notice which read, 'There are no fits of depression in this house. We are not interested in the possibility of defeat'.

His opposite number in Australia, John Curtin, said early in 1942 when facing the advancing Japanese, *'Nobody worries about being a few goals down at half-time'.*

It would be a pity if the spirit which helped to win a war did not remain to enable people to win the peace and make worthwhile the sacrifices made on the battlefield!

Then it is important to empower people and give them a sense of common cause and achievement. The manager or leader who can do that will be a real winner. There can be no leaders without followers.

Field Marshall Montgomery said of Winston Churchill:

> *'There was a certain magnificence about him which turned the lead of other men into gold'.*

As a wartime leader Churchill managed to imbue his countrymen and women with a sense of purpose. They faced a common danger and joined in a common cause.

Of course, Churchill as a wartime leader made some grave mistakes but then leaders often make more mistakes than others simply because leadership involves risk-taking. Those who make no mistakes probably make no advances either.

The effective manager/leader should endeavour to make all his or her workers feel like 'managers' and 'leaders' in the sense that they share the dignity of responsibility and a sense of having a stake in the organisation. True winners are secure enough in themselves to be ready to share power and paradoxically increase their own influence in the process.

Chapter Twelve

Management by Values

WILLIAM TEMPLE said that the modern world was like a shop window into which someone had crept and mischievously changed all the price labels. As a result, things of little worth were highly priced and things of great value grossly under-priced. It was an apt description.

A British politician declared that the language of priorities was the religion of his party. Now whether or not he was justified in his claim there can be no doubt that we all need to speak the 'language of priorities'; in other words we need to put first things first.

I have no particular brief or desire to criticise the late Elvis Presley. Although at the end he was a rather pathetic figure, there is no doubt that he brought a lot of pleasure to many people—and indeed, through his recordings, he still does. He was undoubtedly gifted which was why he was called 'the king'. However, it gave me cause to pause and reflect when I read that for one night's appearance on a television programme and for singing a couple of songs he received more than the annual salary of the President of the United States at that time.

The writer also estimated that the sum he received would, at the time, have paid the annual salary of 25 school teachers, 42 ministers of religion or 63 farm hands. It would have provided a year's training for more than thirty nurses, given more than 125 young people a year in college, stocked ten third world hospitals with drugs and similar necessities or fed 3,000 refugee children for a year. Now I was not in a position to verify the figures and could only take them on trust with some reservations, but, whether strictly accurate or not, they are generally indicative of the very mixed values in our society.

Of course, it comes down to supply and demand. Economic factors call the tune. The values of the market-place will often dictate policy, but may not other values call for consideration also? In fact, may not keeping our society 'human' depend upon our taking them into account?

The Age newspaper in Melbourne reported the visit of Professor S.K. Chakraborty, convenor of the Indian Institute of Management centre for human values. He claimed that the new tenets of management needed to be tempered by the old wisdom of religion and philosophy if the planet—and its businesses—were to survive. Without values and ethics to underpin their activities, individuals and businesses increasingly threatened humanity's long-term survival.

The professor believed that management by values must replace the 'anything that works' gospel preached in pursuit of goals such as increased market share. According to *The Age* report, he said:

'If exploitation of one individual by another be treated as unethical why not exploitation of Nature by man, especially when it is spurred by greed not need.

'Individuals must take responsibility for their actions in business as in other areas of life. If the cultivation of higher values strengthens human values like gratitude, caring, a work ethic, honesty, forgiveness, humility and so on we see no reason why they should not improve organisational effectiveness.

'Team-work, co-ordination and communication all suffer when organisations are not based on healthy human values. People are beginning to talk about values in management and that is a positive sign. At least, people are starting to listen and management schools are beginning to launch a course or two in ethics.

'We do not rule out the need for competition but we do say that unless healthy human values are in good shape and in proper place competition is bound to produce unethical business decisions. We regard sound human values as the basic foundation on which competition can remain healthy and useful.'

Does the wise man from the east have something to say to us in the west? He probably does. The greatest values in the universe are inside not outside human personality and if we ignore them we may bring ourselves and our environment crashing down.

Creative Tension

Of course, the tension between financial viability and ethical considerations is sometimes very great, but handled wisely it can be a creative tension. There were slave owners who felt that they would face financial ruin when people like William Wilberforce sought to end the slave trade, but few people looking back would not say that emancipation had to happen and that in the long run, it was compatible with economic prosperity for the population at large.

Management by values puts a human face on administration and this book contains many references to people who have combined good business sense with proper respect for decent values. Such a person is Irene, the executive director of an up-to-date north American hospital with a staff of about eight hundred.

During a period of recession the financial pressures upon her were enormous but she never lost sight of human factors. Although extremely astute in her management she remained people-orientated. Her staff knew it and as a result she had far fewer personnel problems than might have been expected. Because of the kind of atmosphere she helped to create patients often commented that there was something different about the hospital.

I was a member of the hospital's board of management and could see things from that vantage point, but at one time I was also a patient when, clad in the unflattering anonymity of a hospital gown, I could gauge actions and reactions from a patient's perspective.

I wondered whether Irene's approach to people had anything to do with the fact that a few years earlier she had herself been a patient with what could have been a terminal disease. That may have helped her get fundamental values into focus. Be that as it may, management by values involves having empathy with other people and a healthy respect for their point of view. In fact, it means being truly human!

Chapter Thirteen

Managing—Upwards and Downwards

PETER WICKENS has written:

> *'We have become managerial "fad surfers". We ride the wave of the latest business fad until it is beached, and then paddle out again seeking the next big wave and the exhilarating sense that we can solve anything. Many though have come to realise that while the fad may temporarily elate, its lasting impact is doubtful'.*

Some fads may fail because they concentrate on processes and do not give enough attention to people. They define success too narrowly and substitute little ambitions for larger ideals. Often current catch phrases will prove to be simplistic and the realities of situations much more complex.

For example, a one-time colleague of mine was in the habit of saying, 'People are more important than principles'. On first hearing that sounded fine to me, but later I had reason to realise that a lot depended on what principles were in mind. Discard some principles and people would be the first casualties.

A recurring theme in some books I have read recently is that to succeed you have to make the boss look good and practically ignore what subordinates may think. Like many half-truths or near truths this has a seductive simplicity. Of course, bosses will value those who can help them to appear better and do better and they may well promote their helpers accordingly. In common with others, bosses like to be confirmed in their opinions and so may appreciate those who will simply echo their own views. But sycophants should beware. Give poor advice even as an echo of the boss' own thoughts and when things go wrong you will be first to cop the blame!

Then it may not be wise to assume that the boss is entirely without perception and unable to detect when he is being manipulated by the blatant self-interest of a subordinate. Toadies stick out a mile and may be used but are hardly respected. Respect (including self-respect) belongs to those who have larger loyalties—to the organisation and its mission, for example.

Wise bosses appreciate people who, in the right way and in the right place, will courteously put across a point of view that is different, accepting that the final decision is not theirs. Some of us have reason to be grateful to colleagues who have saved us from ourselves and from making foolish mistakes. There can be both loyalty and integrity and in the long run that is likely to be a winning combination.

Winners try to avoid ever taking a problem to their superior without a suggested solution. While observing the limits of their authority they are not into passing the buck—up or down. They are not seen to be part of the problem but part of the solution to it. Self-seekers should consider that if they go up and their organisation goes down they may be little advantaged. In the end, narrow self-interest may be self-defeating.

For or Against

Some people seem to be born with a permanent seat on the opposition. They are only balanced in that they have a chip on both shoulders! If something is official policy then they are against it. If the boss wants it then they don't. Such folk are sometimes so anxious to demonstrate that they are not 'sucking up' to the boss (to use a common if unpleasant expression) that they go to the other extreme and may show less than the normal courtesies due. That is both wrong and rather foolish.

In general, following the directions of superiors will be right and proper and making them 'look good' no bad thing. But entirely ignoring the feelings of subordinates will hardly be wise.

After all, the executive office may not be entirely sound proof and if the boss hears rumblings of discontent from the lower office floors he may well ask what is happening and why. Moreover, every executive should seek to be kind to the people he meets on the way up the corporate ladder. Apart from anything else, he may meet those same people on the way down!

In a situation where I was 'number two' in the organisation I often had to communicate decisions after consultation with the boss. One person who was a member of staff at that time later told me that people never knew whether the decisions were really mine or the those of the boss. I replied that folk were not meant to know. Behind closed doors there might be disagreement but outside those doors there was solidarity. (The only possible exception would have been on a matter of serious principle which fortunately never arose.)

Later, when I was in the senior position I always had an understanding with my principal colleague. My door was open. We met frequently and worked closely on a basis of mutual trust. I never deliberately did anything behind the back of my colleague and expected the same consideration from him. If there was a difference of opinion we talked it through and almost always came to a common conclusion, although occasionally I had to overrule.

I made it clear that my colleague was quite free to be frank and express views different from mine. Just as in the Westminster system of government we value and pay people to form a 'loyal opposition' so I appreciated hearing alternative points of view even if I could not always accept them. However, when in private conference a decision had been made, public loyalty and solidarity was expected. Failure in this respect would have made it possible for any Tom, Dick or Harry to 'divide and rule'.

Sometimes a leader needs and should appreciate a colleague who, without fear or favour, will communicate reactions and responses among staff, for example. At the same time staff may need someone who will be a good go-between and fairly represent their position to authority. In wise management— upward and downward—the careful balance of loyalty and integrity is important.

If a person in an organisation expects others to accept his or her authority then they will need to accept the authority of those above them. Fair enough? While flatter administrative structures may take the place of hierarchical arrangements to some extent, the principle of authority must remain. A subordinate should still give proper place to the boss but by the same token a boss should give sufficient space to the subordinate.

Much depends on how we define success and how much we are prepared to pay for it. In my book, mutual respect for people as people is the essence of good management.

Chapter Fourteen

What About Communicating?

WE HAVE lived through a communications revolution, yet those who are in the know say that 'we haven't seen anything yet'. We've got used to the idea of receiving messages by means of satellites in space; we take it for granted that letters from the other side of the world can reach us by fax in a matter of seconds.

The problem seems to be getting information from one office to the next. We can plug into information from around the globe but try finding out what's happening about extra places in the employees car park or fixing the plumbing in the ladies washroom or rumours of reorganisation and you may come up against a wall of silence!

Strangely enough, there can be a communications breakdown even in small organisations. The left hand may not know what the right hand is doing. People who see each other every day may be so near and yet so far in some respects.

Sometimes it seems that the people who know the least about a company are some of those who work for it, even at head office! Public relations consultants may have expensive strategies for disseminating information to those outside the firm but what about improving the nervous system within the structure? It may be said that the tail shouldn't wag the dog but it is too bad if the head doesn't even know when the tail has a pain. The need for two-way communication is clear.

So what's the problem? Why is it that there can be a communication breakdown even in sophisticated organisations?

Very often it's nothing more or less than plain thoughtlessness. People in the know don't think of communicating what could and should be common knowledge.

It is said that nature abhors a vacuum and certainly, where there is a lack of information, in no time at all misinformation will be circulating and the rumour mill will be working overtime. Staff unrest can easily arise out of garbled reports or wrong impressions.

Of course, in any organisation there will be information which is not for general distribution. Some matters need to be kept confidential and for very good reasons, but having said that, openness and frankness can very often clear the air and improve the atmosphere in a workplace. Winners know that if there is nothing to hide there is no point in playing out a cloak and dagger role. Tell it like it is—and why it is!

Sometimes it may be found that providing information is not the same as communicating. Information overload can be a problem. The likelihood of a document being read may be in inverse ratio to its length. (My desk—and the person behind it —has sometimes groaned under the weight of documents lacking the thoughtful provision of summaries. Even with speed reading it is possible to get bogged down.)

Breakdowns in Communication

There will always be people who hear what they want to hear and don't take in all that they should. The carefully drafted head office memo may never get past middle management or the vital information from where the action is may not reach or be understood by those with ultimate responsibility. In an imperfect world there will be some breakdowns of communication but they ought to be far fewer than they often are.

One of the roles of top management is to communicate an inspiring vision for the organisation. In this the mission statement may be important as long as it is not allowed to become an empty bit of company 'liturgy'. Top management should embody the vision rather than merely give lip service to it. As an old adage had it, 'What I live by, I impart'. Influence flows downhill as a rule and unless senior staff are perceived to be 'sold' on policy there will be little likelihood of others endorsing and supporting it.

If major changes are envisaged in an organisation then ways and means of communicating these should be worked out. In one situation I initiated a large scale structural re-organisation—the first for many decades. This followed the report of outside consultants commissioned by my predecessor and the findings of an internal commission which took submissions from more than a thousand interested parties with sixteen resource groups meeting in different parts of the very large country. As an expatriate, I was particularly concerned that those with long-time local knowledge should have adequate input and that all should be kept informed of progress at every stage.

The main changes recommended meant co-ordination of operations locally and devolution of authority nationally so that more decisions could be taken closer to the action.

There were those who had fears of what the changes would mean for them but the appointment of a full-time facilitator helped a great deal. Over a couple of years he travelled considerable distances in order to meet individuals and groups, allay fears and also convey concerns back to the administration. As a result many problems were solved even before they arose.

Of course, where possible, decision-makers should take opportunities of meeting with staff personally and becoming acquainted with problems at first hand. Where that is impossible I have found that the sending out of personalised letters or the preparation of information videos may help, together with the securing of genuine feedback.

None of us likes to be in the dark about matters which affect us vitally and it makes sense for people at all levels in an organisation to seek to improve the communication network. This is one way in which we can show that we care about each other as people. Does it take time and cost money? So be it. The investment will be well worthwhile. Frustration and aggravation arising out of lack of information would probably cost much more.

Chapter Fifteen

Committed to Excellence

HOW MUCH do we value a commitment to excellence? Let me tell you about a time when I would have thought it especially important. I had to undergo coronary artery surgery. I knew that the surgeon was a fellow Rotarian and said to be very clever. I also knew that he was very busy and that I would be one of many patients upon whom he would operate.

I certainly hoped that his professional commitment to excellence wouldn't slip when he had my heart in his hands. I didn't want to be a mistake to be buried! For a surgeon, I might be one more case, but for me his commitment to medical excellence was a matter of life and death.

Our responsibilities may be very different and yet in some ways our commitment to excellence will also impinge upon the well-being and happiness of other folk. It will indicate the kind of people we are too.

If the colloquial Aussie phrase, 'She'll be right, mate' is an expression of cheerful optimism, as it usually is, all well and good. But if it were ever to indicate a couldn't-care-less approach to life and work then that would be too bad.

Some years ago John Gardner, a former head of the Carnegie Corporation, wrote a book which he called *Excellence* with the thought provoking sub-title, *'Can We be Equal and Excellent Too?'* While valuing all that is good about egalitarianism we mustn't forget that we need the tall poppies of excellence.

"The search for excellence is linked to self-respect"

We rightly admire sportsmen and women who are committed to physical excellence and achieve great feats as climbers, runners or swimmers. One such is Dr Roger Bannister who was the first man to run a mile in under four minutes. He has said that 'most of the citizenry are comfortably unfit' and he is probably right. However, super athletes like Bannister inspire lesser mortals to jog and watch their diet and be the best that they can be.

In Exeter, England, I knew a young man called Alan. He was a painter and decorator by trade but his special strength was in swimming. As a possible contender for his country's Olympic team his dedication was awesome. Early and late he was at the pool, perfecting his strokes and always striving to lop point something of a second off his time. In the water, Alan was poetry in motion. Later his sense of commitment was channelled into the form of community service which has become his life's vocation.

In Melbourne, Australia, I have a young friend called Trudi. Her ambition is to become a concert pianist and as early as six o'clock in the morning she can be found at her church where she has the use of a piano. Hour after hour she practises. Her goal is excellence and nothing but the best can be good enough.

When I was living in Toronto, Canada, I sometimes shared lunch with Ian, an academic turned entrepreneur. He had built up a business producing leisure wear of the highest quality and durability. He had also developed a flair for marketing with humorous and eye-catching publicity. In that he reminded me of the verse:

> *He who whispers down a well*
> *About the goods he has to sell,*
> *Will never reap the golden dollars*
> *Like he who lifts his head and hollers!*

But Ian's successful business was built on something more substantial than publicity gimmicks—customer satisfaction. He had a commitment to excellence and as one who bought goods from him I can testify to their enduring quality.

The Prizes for Excellence

Many of the benefits of life which we enjoy are due to those who have been committed to excellence in the arts, sciences or commercial world—people for whom only the best was good enough, winners whose prizes we have shared in one way or another.

The word 'excellence' is defined in The Concise Oxford Dictionary as 'surpassing merit'. It sets a standard and assumes that there are levels which are less than the best, poorer than they could be and perhaps less than worthy.

What we are thinking about is superlative but not static. The people who do excellently are usually the people who always want to do more excellently. They know that there are always higher heights to scale and deeper depths to plumb. I recall a fine public speaker who was asked to name his best speech. He said, 'My next one!'

While excellence may be linked to special gifts it is especially the domain of the highly motivated. As a rule it doesn't come easily. It has a price on it and demands dedication.

In a book on the art of management, Ted W. Engstrom and Edward R. Dayton (to whom I am indebted) suggested that the first 80 per cent of an excellent result may come easily. The next 15 per cent may be hard and the last 5 per cent can cost the earth.

A commitment to excellence may arise out of a sense of responsibility to other people as, for example, a nurse's responsibility to patients or a teacher's responsibility to pupils or a businessman's responsibility to customers. Shoddy work would be a betrayal of trust.

But for many people the search for excellence is also linked to self-respect. They have to do their best in order to be true to themselves and satisfy the monitor within them. The thought of having done a bad job would haunt them. On the other hand, the knowledge that they have done their very best is reward in itself and makes them winners even if the world doesn't always crown them as such.

The American poet James Russell Lowell wrote:

Life is a leaf of paper white
Whereon each one of us may write
His word or two, then comes night.

Greatly begin! though thou hast time
But for a line, be that sublime.
Not failure but low aim is crime.

Chapter Sixteen

Building Trust

IN MANY sections of society there has been an erosion of trust. Bad publicity has affected many professions so that, for example, financiers, priests, police, bankers, lawyers and others often command less respect than they once did. Sadly, it only takes one or two publicised bad cases to reduce respect for a whole profession.

None have suffered more than politicians whose credibility ratings seem to be at an all-time low. If I focus on them it is not because, as people, they are nesessarily any worse than others, but just that their activities are more public and that their special privileges do carry special responsibilities.

Henry Kissinger is reported to have said that 90 per cent of politicians are giving the other 10 per cent a bad name! As a politician himself, I am sure that he spoke with his tongue in his cheek. In fact, through the years I have had dealings with many politicians who have struck me not as being particularly self-seeking but as public-spirited and genuinely concerned about the less fortunate folk in society. I would like to think that they are representative of many others.

By way of illustration, in Canada I had personal dealings with the Premier of one of the Provinces. He impressed me immensely by the brilliance of his intellect. Even more, I appreciated the honesty and openness with which he was ready, in his own home, to discuss the matter of concern to both of us. Because of economic necessity he had to implement some extremely rigorous policies, but because of his known integrity and disarming frankness those policies were accepted and he was returned to power with a clear mandate from the electorate. Who says that good guys can't win?

Image-wise, politicians may sometimes suffer from their treatment by the media, but having made allowance for that, 'ya-yaroo' exchanges in parliament can hardly be expected to enhance the dignity and standing of those elected as leaders. Sometimes behaviour in 'the House' is such as would not be tolerated by a self-respecting school principal in a playground.

We could do with a few more politicians who would break the mould and be ready to make generous references to political opponents or sometimes concede that the other side has done something right. Privately this is done, but if done publicly it might well have surprising results. Saying that everything your opponent does is wrong doesn't carry weight. Giving credit where credit is due would actually add credibility to criticism when it was made.

A Way of Earning Trust

Being fair to others is certainly a way of earning trust for oneself. Let me tell you about Keith, an Australian who, as a young married man with children, found himself in a rather boring routine job. By dint of hard work over several years, he qualified as a lawyer and specialised in industrial legislation, eventually rising to a very senior position—equivalent to that of a judge—in the field of industrial arbitration. The welfare of thousands of workers and the allocation of millions of dollars of capital hung on his decisions. Sometimes he was subject to pressure—even a bribe. True, he had the authority of the law behind him but it was equally important that he should enjoy the trust of the parties with which he dealt.

By 'playing it straight down the middle' and dealing without fear or favour he earned acceptance so that usually, even parties who were disappointed by a judgement, tended to accept it rather than appeal, feeling that it had been delivered in good faith and that on a future occasion the judgement could well go their way.

"*Building trust depends on trustworthiness.*"

In Britain I came to know a man who was the general secretary of one of the largest trade unions in the country and, at one time, national chairman of the Labour party. He was dubbed 'the militant moderate'. There was nothing mealy-mouthed about John. He had a rugged eloquence born out of experience in Scottish shipyards and as a local preacher in his chosen church. People would not always agree with him but nearly everyone felt that they could trust him. His principles were not for bending. Not surprisingly, he counted among his friends many far removed from either his political or religious persuasion. He was a man who helped to build trust often where that was not easy but very important, nonetheless.

A few years ago I had an interview with the chief executive of one of the largest banks in the country where I was working. My organisation was in dispute with the bank and there was the prospect of expensive legal proceedings and considerable publicity unwanted by both parties. I had previously met the man socially and had taken the trouble to check him out through people who knew him, as well as in other ways. My instincts and my information agreed: this man was likely to be concerned about what was right and not merely about who was right. In fact, that proved to be the case.

We had both been briefed on the complicated matters in hand but it made a difference that we were able to meet in an atmosphere of mutual trust.

Smart Cookies

It may go without saying that building trust depends upon trustworthiness. In addition to our having an acceptable degree of competence in our field people need to know that we will be 'fair dinkum' and straightforward in all our dealings. I have known folk who may have been described as 'smart cookies' with a degree of admiration but a tinge of mistrust. There has been the feeling that while not actually dishonest they were not quite up front. For that reason a board might be inclined to scrutinise their submissions more carefully, in case there was some hidden agenda. That could have been to their loss.

I once had dealings with a man who wrote letters in such a way that they were capable of more than one interpretation. Apparently he thought that in certain circumstances that might work to his advantage. In fact it only made people wary.

I have learnt that it is possible to tell the truth with intent to deceive. I mean, we may present facts in such a way that a completely false impression is conveyed. Smart? Not in the long run. Real winners don't sell their birthright of credibility for some short-term advantage.

It is important to realise that by the way we act we may not only build (or fail to build) trust in ourselves but in our firm or our particular profession. Others stand or fall by what we do. In turn, we gain or lose acceptance according to the way in which others conduct themselves.

As a young man I was sent to work in a small town in England and found it very difficult because of the conduct of my predecessors. Fortunately, in many other situations I have enjoyed trust and acceptance on the strength of those who have gone before me. Didn't John Donne say something about no man being an island?

Some people are slow to give credit to those who have gone before them. Ask them how things are going and they will reply, 'Things are all right now, but when I first came everything was in a terrible mess!' That may or may not be true but sometimes such folk always feel the need to put down their predecessor in order to build themselves up.

It is gratifying when folk are big enough to pay tribute to good work done before their arrival on a scene—or after their departure, come to that.

I appreciated the tribute to his Australian predecessor by the world leader of a well-known religious movement recognised for its social welfare work. He wrote:

> *The light shone through him. The windows of his soul were always clean, and his outlook was high and wide. There were no dark holes and corners in his character. Yet those*

> *who supposed this unoffending guilelessness was an easy*
> *prey to the more worldly-wise, soon discovered their error!'*

People like that build believability into their institutions and professions and make the world an altogether better place in which to live.

Chapter Seventeen

The Best Policy?

WHEN I LIVED in Canada I had contacts with one of the most well-known and colourful characters in that country. Ed Mervish —self-styled as 'Honest Ed'—has a huge cut-price emporium which is as garish as could be imagined. He also has a chain of restaurants where the food is good but the decor unusual, to say the least. Ed is a very wealthy man who has bought theatres around the world—including the famous Old Vic in London, England.

He himself is flamboyantly theatrical, but very likeable—and generous, as I have reason to know. He told me:

'The only thing about saying that you're honest is that there will always be people out to prove that you're not'.

Nevertheless he has built his very considerable business on a claim to be honest.

I have known many others who, in more modest ways perhaps, have sought to build on a basis of fair dealing—and have proved that it can be done.

By way of contrast, the television channels have provided plenty of illustrations of people who have gambled with other people's money, have lost and yet still managed to secure for themselves a lush lifestyle. They may have fled to their 'island in the sun' but behind them has been a trail of little people whose hopes have been blighted and whose lives have been blasted by financial ruin. The worst part has been that some of these characters have not merely been the victims of financial misfortune with a genuine concern for those who have been implicated in their difficulties; they have apparently been quite unconcerned about those who have suffered because of their mistakes, with no apologies escaping their lips. Their own health and happiness has been their only apparent concern.

Such so-called 'entrepreneurs' epitomise the attitude sometimes expressed by servicemen in the war in such phrases as 'Blow you, Jack, I'm inboard'.

Are such people winners? Not to my mind. It has been said that 'gentlemen' are those who put more into the common stock than they take out and in my book such people, men or women, are the real winners whatever their cash balances may be in the end.

Real Honesty

However, there are many who could show that real honesty and good financial rewards can go together, and leave intact the very considerable bonus of self-respect.

Recently, some friends of mine needed work done on their house and sought estimates for this. One contractor was careful to point out work that didn't need to be done, although he could easily have magnified the need to his own possible advantage. Not surprisingly, he got the job because my friends felt, instinctively, that he was honest and straightforward. They were anxious to tell me about this contractor and doubtless told others. In other words, his honesty got him a lot of free advertising by word of mouth.

I enquired about the commercial affairs of a successful Australian businessman. Broadly speaking, he told me that the matter of questionable deals didn't arise because it was known that he was simply not into such things. He had started straight and that had made it easier for him to go on that way. Far from being an impediment to his business this had actually enhanced it. People knew that he was 'fair dinkum' and if anything were more ready to do deals with him as a result. Incidentally, my independent observations gave me no reason to doubt that what he said was right.

When I worked in New Zealand, I had a good relationship with a fine man who, at one time, held the national franchise for a well-known chain of fast food outlets. He told me that he had been obliged by the parent organisation to maintain the highest standards of quality and cleanliness at all times. Apart from anything else, a world-wide reputation depended on this. The cost of carelessness could be enormous. Any form of dishonesty would also have been out of the question, so far as he was concerned.

I find it encouraging that in the commercial world as well as in many of the professions there is an increasing emphasis on the need for high ethical standards. Any conflict of interests must be declared or it is likely to be exposed very quickly. This may be helped by the fact that we live in an increasingly investigative society in which it seems that nothing is hidden that will not be revealed. The media deserve credit here. While sometimes they may have been unduly intrusive into the private lives of celebrities and even guilty of character assassination, there have been many other situations where their role has helped to keep people honest. The fear of media exposure as well as the fear of the policeman may have been beneficial!

But the salt of society are those who have nothing to fear because they have nothing to hide. The real winners are those who are 'honest in the dark'—that is, whether people know what they are doing or not. They will be honest simply because it is right regardless of whether it pays. For them, honesty is more than a matter of expediency. Their consciences are their 'internal auditors' whose findings matter most of all. It was no lesser genius than Albert Einstein who said:

> *'Try not to be a man of success but rather be a man of value'.*

On that basis, the old adage 'Honesty is the best policy' must always be right. The 'smart alec' may say, 'Do others before they do you', but the good person (not the same as the 'goody, goody', by the way) prefers to stick with the golden rule: 'Do to others as you would like them to do to you'.

Chapter Eighteen

Opportunity Knocks!

I HAVE heard that the son of a couple I used to know in the United Kingdom walked into a music shop and met a now world famous pop star. As a result, so I am informed, he became the future star's manager almost overnight and in a couple of years, while still young, was a wealthy man. Such stories are the stuff of which dreams are made; they don't usually bear much relation to reality.

Yet, in less spectacular fashion opportunities do present themselves and are taken up by those with eyes to see. Shakespeare wrote:

*'There is a tide in the affairs of men, which, taken at the
flood leads on to fortune'.*

Sometimes, of course, opportunities don't come out of the blue but have to be made.

Think of commercial opportunities. The trick may well be to identify a need and meet it or find a niche in the market and fill it. I have read of two brothers in England who, many years ago, failed their examinations and decided to sell their textbooks. They received so many enquiries that they started a small business which became Foyles, in Charing Cross Road, London, which has been acclaimed as one of the largest bookshops in the world.

A man and wife who are good friends of mine in Scotland discovered that whole libraries of second-hand books could often be picked up for the proverbial song. They also latched on to the fact that in the United States some of those books would fetch relatively high prices. So, although their main business was in a very different line they were not above diversifying and running a profitable sideline exporting second-hand books.

I read about a woman in the United States who advertised that she was ready to listen to anyone talk about anything for a certain number of dollars an hour. She had so many lonely people apply that she had to take on helpers to meet the demand!

Sometimes markets waiting to be opened up may be under our noses. For example, some firms have woken up to the fact that their employees could also be their customers—especially if encouraged with some staff discounts.

Opportunities for Relationships

Opportunities to make worthwhile relationships should not be overlooked. Many a business is bedevilled by poor inter-personal relationships. The 'management proposes therefore the union opposes' theme is still sometimes played out with variations. The problem may be with insensitive management or intransigent labour or a bit of both, but in the end everybody loses.

In one country where I worked a large industry was so affected by chronic industrial difficulties that eventually it lost out to overseas competition and was decimated with a massive loss of jobs.

I wouldn't oversimplify such situations which may be quite complex but they do remind me of a children's story about a donkey who was happily grazing in a paddock until another donkey was put to graze there as well. Feeling that it was being glared at, the newcomer decided to kick up a mound of earth behind which it could feel secure. That led the first donkey to do the same. In fact, the two silly donkeys kicked up so much dirt in order to build their defences that eventually there was little grass left for either to graze upon.

In organisations where barriers exist between management and staff or between different departments every opportunity should be sought to build bridgeheads of friendship. Not with any manipulative motive but with genuine goodwill it should be possible to express sympathy at times of bereavement or congratulations when these would be appropriate. All sorts of social opportunities may be found which will humanise relationships and help to overcome prejudice. It may take time and patience but it will be well worth it. There may still be differences of opinion and competing interests but there need not be the ridiculous rancour which benefits no-one.

Opportunities for self-improvement may also be found. In the middle of an information revolution there is no need for us to be ignorant. To an extent undreamed of by our forefathers we can gain knowledge and thus broaden our outlook and prepare ourselves for whatever the future may bring. Opportunities for acquiring new skills should not be overlooked. In my youth it was generally expected that a person would stay in one trade or profession for the whole of their working life. Now it may be necessary for a man or woman to have two or three different careers in a lifetime. In some ways this may be good but it can also put pressure on people with the burden of making critical choices.

Evaluating Opportunities

In evaluating opportunities there is a need for discernment. What appears to be gold could be fool's gold. What seems like an oasis could be a mirage. There is always a need for cautious courage. Clear thinking is imperative. Sometimes independent advice may be sought—the views of one competent adviser being balanced with those of another. Prudence would indicate that all possible checks be made.

However, opportunities almost inevitably call for decisions. Ultimately, life is in the affirmative; winners can't dither for ever. Chester Wilmot in his book *The Struggle for Europe* told of tense moments on Sunday night, 4th June, 1944, the eve of the invasion of Europe. There was poor visibility and the prediction of deterioration in the weather but postponement of the landings would mean large scale disorganisation. What was to be done? Was this the window of opportunity? The final decision was left until 4.15 am on the Monday morning. The latest weather reports were received, then all eyes turned to General Eisenhower sitting at the end of the table in the Operations Room. The silence was electric, charged with destiny. For almost a minute no-one spoke, then clearly and positively Eisenhower said, 'OK, we'll go!'

We may be grateful that we are not called upon to make decisions as fateful as that one, but in our very much smaller theatre of operations we may have to make choices affecting our own future and perhaps that of others as well. Having done our homework, we can only do our best and leave the rest, make our decision and live with it.

To take advantage of opportunities there will be the need for determination. The door of opportunity often has 'push' on it! Opportunities may come but it may still be necessary to work for success.

Anthony Trollope is a deservedly famous novelist. He had his opportunities but no easy passage. He was an inspector with the Post Office, first in Ireland and then in England and had to travel constantly. He devised a writing pad which he could hold on his knees and wrote the greater part of his early novels while travelling in somewhat unsteady trains.

He was required to go to Egypt on postal business and described his voyage:

> *'As I journeyed across France to Marseilles, and made thence a terribly rough voyage to Alexandria, I wrote my allotted number of pages every day. On this occasion more than once I left my paper on the cabin table, rushing away to be sick in the privacy of my state room. It was February, and the weather was miserable; but still I did my work.'*

Some people have opportunities but lack the determination to make the best of them. Winners determine to do better.

Chapter Nineteen

Accentuate the Positive

I AM PROBABLY 'dated' by the fact that I can remember a popular song with the line, *'You've got to accentuate the positive, eliminate the negative'*. No matter! With the lines of many pop songs it is a case of once heard never remembered, but the idea of having a positive emphasis in life has always appealed to me, which may be why I have remembered the line from the dim and distant past.

It was in 1953 that Norman Vincent Peale first published his famous book, *The Power of Positive Thinking*. The fact that it is still on sale in bookshops is testimony to the enduring value of some of the principles it sets out. Peale wrote:

> *'I certainly do not ignore or minimise the hardships and tragedies of the world but neither do I allow them to dominate. You can permit obstacles to control your mind to the point where they are uppermost and thus become dominating factors in your thought pattern. By learning how to cast them from the mind, by refusing to become mentally subservient to them, and by channelling spiritual power through your thoughts, you can rise above obstacles which ordinarily might defeat you.'*

Would-be winners should take note. I guess that it would not be too hard to write about the power of negative thinking, and it wouldn't be difficult to find examples of the debilitating effect that it can have on individuals and on those with whom they have contact. I came across this in a book by Hugh Redwood:

> '"A single grain of indigo will colour a ton of water" says Professor Thomson. Which is science's way of warning us how infectious the blues can be'.

Fair enough, pessimism may be pervasive, but the same is true of optimism. One positive thinker can lift the morale of a whole company. So let's give our vote to the winners not the whiners!

We Should Seek to Have Positive Attitudes Towards People

Now of course there are plenty of con artists in the world. There are those who would 'take us for a ride', given half a chance. But that is no reason for us to take a jaundiced view of the whole human race. It is better to be taken in once in a while than to dismiss a lot of people who could do us good.

Some people are locked up in themselves and find it hard to open up to others. They are friendless because they appear unfriendly. The problem is that they are not ready to risk taking people on trust. They cannot believe that strangers may simply be friends that they have not met before.

Now of course, I am not advocating gullibility or the suspension of the critical faculty. I am simply saying that we should be more ready to give people the benefit of the doubt and take a positive attitude. And often, although not always, the positive attitude will evoke a positive response.

It may be worth an experiment. We can go to the office or the shop with a grouchy approach and as likely as not we will get grumpy rejoinders. On the other hand, a warm, cheerful and positive attitude may help to thaw even the frosty souls around the place. It is amazing what a difference positive goodwill and open friendliness can make even in a tough business meeting! At least, it's worth a try!

The home is the assembly line of national character and certainly a place where positive attitudes are needed, particularly because of the effect they can have on the children.

With regard to our influence on the young W. A. Peterson has written:

*'When we encircle them with love they will be loving.
When we are thankful for life's blessings they will be
thankful. When we express friendliness they will be
friendly. When we speak words of praise they will praise
others. When we set an example of honesty our children
will be honest. When we practice tolerance they will be
tolerant. When we confront misfortune with a gallant
spirit they will learn to live bravely. When our lives affirm
faith in the enduring values of life they will rise above
doubt and scepticism. We can't stand there pointing our
finger to the heights we want our children to scale. We must
start climbing, and they will follow!'*

There is a lot of validity in those words although, of course,
apart from our influence, there are other causes and other effects
with which we may have to reckon.

We Should Seek to Have a Positive Attitude Towards our Circumstances

The way we look at life can make a lot of difference to our
approach. One person may look at a draught board and see it as
black with white squares while someone else may see it as white
with black squares. So also, different people see similar
circumstances in different ways.

Every time some people fall down they pick up something,
every time they lose they learn. Such folk are winners, whatever
happens. For them, the best is always yet to be.

Lloyd C. Douglas, author of deservedly famous novels such as
The Robe and *The Big Fisherman*, tells of going to visit an old
philosopher who had fallen on hard times. He was living in a
musty attic at the top of rickety stairs. Lloyd Douglas greeted
him with the question, 'What's the good news today?'

By way of reply, the old man went to a gong hanging in a
corner of the room. He struck it and said:

'That's 'A'. It was 'A' yesterday. It will be 'A' tomorrow or in
a thousand years. The noise from the street is awful. The piano

downstairs is out of tune. But that's 'A', and that's the good news'.

With a positive attitude we will always be able to find something that's constant and reassuring, even in the most depressing circumstances.

I would think that it must have been difficult, and almost impossible, to be positive in the concentration camp at Auschwitz. If ever there was a 'no-win' situation that would have been it. Yet, in that place of horror a Jewish prisoner scrawled the following words on a wall:

> *'I believe in the sun even when it is not shining. I believe in love even when I cannot feel it. I believe in God even when he is silent'.*

The human spirit that could triumph like that was a winner indeed. So what is our problem?

Chapter Twenty

Winners Have Energy

THERE are times when most of us feel that we have a personal energy crisis. It may be because we are unwell and need to see a doctor, or it may be that we are getting older and need to recognise that although our 'get-up-and-go' may not have all got up and gone, we simply don't have the physical stamina we once had.

Sometimes a sense of exhaustion may be due to nothing more than failure to take time out for recreation. To ignore the old commandment about taking a day of rest may not only be wrong religiously but foolish physically.

However, sometimes we fail to generate energy because we lack a certain vital spark. Some years ago I knew a young lady who always seemed to be tired, so much so that I wondered whether she was ill. One day I happened to be in her home when she came in from work. Immediately, she subsided into a chair. She had endured a gruelling day at her place of employment and was far too tired to help her mother lay the table cloth or anything like that.

Then came a knock at the front door. A certain young man was enquiring whether the young lady was free that evening. Was she free? Talk about a transformation! The tiredness fell off like a crumpled garment; dull eyes began to sparkle; listlessness gave way to instant vitality. She tripped along to the front door to talk with the young man and, as far as I could ascertain, made arrangements to go for a long cycle ride that evening. She had found instant energy!

Haven't we all seen the same sort of thing? Couldn't we all tell similar stories—including some against ourselves?

Many a husband is far too tired of an evening to wipe a dish but mention his favourite programme on the television or his special hobby and he is tired no longer. I know that there are some things for which I am rarely too tired but on the other hand the very thought of some jobs makes me feel dead beat!

One thing therefore becomes clear: lacking some compelling interest or motivation we will often feel exhausted long before our physical strength is really used up. It is not that our physical energy has run out; we have only to touch the button of self-interest to prove that. The problem is that in our minds and spirits we have become jaded and wearied by worry or monotony.

Keeping Going

I have known apparently frail people who, faced with special circumstances such as the sickness of a family member, have done without sleep and gone on and on with devoted labour. Others have rightly said that their spirits have kept them going. Without doubt, devotion, dedication or an absorbing interest can call up unsuspected reserves. The will to win may be like the vital spark in a motor car.

But in addition to generating energy we need to learn how to conserve it. Emotional energy may be wasted by worry or dissipated by animosity or bitterness. Hugh Redwood wrote, 'Don't nurse a grievance, teach it to walk!' He had a point there. We spend emotional vitality fretting about something or another but it doesn't get us anywhere. It is like revving up a car with the clutch engaged. Or we work ourselves up and run ourselves down rehearsing the bitter things we are going to say to the boss—although, in reality, we might not dare.

Just as a dripping tap can waste hot water so our energy reserves can be depleted by the way we think even as we are driving our car or walking in the street. The answer is to have some corrective thoughts handy to drop into our consciousness when we catch ourselves wasting our emotional strength. We could go through a little mental check-list of the good things in our lives—like health, a good family, sufficient money to live on or whatever. Or we might give our minds to positive action that might be taken—anything that will divert our minds from futile or even self-destructive thinking.

I recall a couplet by Josiah Conder:

'O to live exempt from care, by the energy of prayer'.

Apart from theological implications, that means that instead of wearing ourselves out with anxiety we should draw on such spiritual resources as are available to us.

It is not only important to generate energy and conserve it; we need to be wise in deploying it. I once spoke to a highly intelligent woman who had a repetitive job on the assembly line of a factory. Hundreds of times a day she repeated the same simple procedure which would have been within the capability of a small child. I remember thinking that such a job would drive me crazy and without saying as much I asked the woman what she thought about all day. She told me that because her work only required a small amount of her mental capacity she used the balance in creative mental activity of one kind or another. She was into useful community service for young people and would spend her spare thought on planning various new activities for the kids.

In his book *Taken on Trust* Terry Waite tells of his 1,763 days as a hostage, four years of which were in solitary confinement. Although under awful pressure he used the time to recollect his life in sequence from childhood onwards. In a sense he wrote his autobiography in his mind, although denied the longed for materials to set it down in writing. He was a winner because he was able to use his time and energy in a creative way despite unimaginable privations. Nothing was wasted.

What counts in a car is what happens where the tyre bites the road. So too with human beings, what counts is not only the energy we generate but what we are able to do with it. We too need to be fuel efficient! There should be maximum effectiveness with minimum weariness, rather than the reverse.

Chapter Twenty-One

Watch Your Style

BY DEFINITION, good leaders must know how to win, but the manner in which they lead and their styles are likely to vary greatly.

Some will tend to be dictatorial or authoritarian and, in certain circumstances, that is just what is needed. For example, it is difficult to imagine military operations being conducted on completely democratic lines. In the heat of battle there may be no time to set up a committee—which has been described as 'a body which keeps minutes and can waste hours!' It is likely to be a case of 'orders are orders'.

When I was young I worked under a very dynamic and indeed effective 'boss'. On reflection, I guess he was authoritarian although admirable in many ways. I have since learnt that his private policy was, 'Work them hard and tell them nothing'—an approach which, I suspect, would be far less acceptable in these days when a much more open approach seems right! Still, it worked then.

Some in key positions always prefer to go by the book, meticulously. In every situation they will feel that it is safer to play by the rules and follow the policy laid down. That way at least there is likely to be consistency in administration. Departure from strict adherence to rules can certainly cause subsequent embarrassment. I recall a former member of staff who sued for alleged wrongful dismissal although the action which had been taken was strictly within the terms under which he had been working. He lost the case, but his counsel was able to cite instances when a previous administration had departed from the 'rules', which was embarrassing.

The Pressure of Precedent

Many is the time in administration when my first impulse has been to grant a request and then I have had cause to pause and consider what precedent I might be setting up for the future. However, there may be times when circumstances demand a degree of flexibility in interpretation of policy. Justice in square blocks may not seem to fit a case. What then?

There are those who usually prefer to let matters take their course. Their line is, 'Don't trouble trouble until trouble troubles you'. If something isn't broken to the point of complete breakdown why fix it? Of course, that kind of leadership is hardly leadership at all. It is certainly not pro-active and barely reactive at times.

Some opt for the consultative approach whether it is the required procedure or not. This may not be the quickest method but it is likely to ensure that more people 'own' the course of action decided upon. In western countries especially, this style may have become more acceptable in recent decades. By involving people in decision-making greater co-operation may be expected. In earlier years I was sometimes called in for 'consultations' only to be told what had already been decided. Does that still happen? Such 'stooge committees' are less common nowadays—I hope!

Of course, different styles may suit different organisations with different operations at different times and in different places. Having worked in various parts of the world, I have learnt that the approach favoured in one place may be less acceptable elsewhere. So, while working within the broad framework of management principles and organisational procedures, it may also be necessary to take account of local sensitivities and circumstances.

For that reason, although every leader may have his or her own characteristic style it may be necessary to modify it at different times and in different circumstances—without sacrificing any fundamental principles, be it said. There should be continuity of principle but adaptation of method and approach.

Apart from trying to be a practitioner I have been a life-long observer of management and leadership styles and I have been fascinated to see the widely different ways in which people have approached their tasks. I have seen very different people succeed but in very different ways.

For example, recently I visited the Australian 'headquarters' of a successful firm with branches in various overseas countries. It is housed in a fairly nondescript, if not run-down house which is considered adequate for the purpose. The founder and 'boss' of the multi-million dollar business chooses to dress casually and occupies one of the smallest rooms as an office. He is quite happy to make the coffee and put the garbage bins out, as required. Everybody is very casual but apparently the operation works well, which is what matters.

Sure, he is a 'nice guy'—but so is the boss of a very different organisation who sits behind his big desk in his large office, well protected by a secretary, a receptionist and a security system, which in his situation may well be necessary.

To the question, 'Which way is best?' the answer is, 'It all depends on what is appropriate in a given situation'. Style will always be a very individual thing, but in the end it is character which counts. The test of management is one, whether it enables the organisation to fulfill its mission and achieve its goals, and two, whether it is liberating, enabling and dignifying for those engaged in the operation. Nice guys in management may vary in their approaches but they all seek this 'win-win' result.

Increasingly, it is being recognised that effective organisations take good care of their human resources. If the staff feel fulfilled, appreciated and properly rewarded then there is more chance that the function of the company will be fulfilled also, which is not surprising really!

Chapter Twenty-Two

Winning With Words

I FIRST became aware of the fascination of words when, as a boy at school, I had to learn Coleridge's poem Kubla Khan and particularly, the lines:

> In Xanadu did Kubla Khan
> A stately pleasure dome decree:
> Where Alph, the sacred river ran
> Through caverns measureless to man
> Down to a sunless sea.

The words may not affect you but they had an almost hypnotic effect on me as a youngster.

The effect of words on people can be incalculable. While on a visit to Norway I heard of how much the words of Winston Churchill meant to people in occupied Europe during the war. He mobilised the English language in such a way that people were roused from apathy and despair and lifted to tremendous heights of human endeavour.

In this chapter I want to consider how we can win with words even though there may be nothing Churchillian about us. It may be unlikely that any of our phrases will become part of the history of literature, yet they may be effective for all that.

Let me say something about the *personal word*. As a teenager I was in a gathering where vocations were being discussed. A woman whispered in my ear, 'What about you, Wesley?' For her it may have been a question asked and forgotten in minutes but somehow I was provoked into thinking seriously about what my life's work should be. More than twenty years later I told the woman of the effect of her question and, to say the least, she was flabbergasted.

Coming at the right moment, a word of encouragement—even on the telephone—can mean a mighty lot.

For many years as a senior executive I phoned hundreds of key staff and retirees with a Christmas greeting and an enquiry after their health. The calls were not usually of more than half a minute's duration each—although I tried not to sound too hurried. However, there were indications that the gesture was appreciated and helped people to feel that management was not too remote or removed. In any case, using one's position to bring even a little encouragement seemed no bad thing.

Use Sensitive Words

There can be value in a sensitive word at a time of bereavement or personal tragedy, for example. Sometimes we are so frightened of saying the wrong thing that we fail to say the right thing. The need is for the courage to speak on occasion and the wisdom to employ the eloquence of silence at other times.

We should always make our words as palatable as possible for after all we never know when we may have to eat them! Of course, often it is not only what we say but the way in which we say it that makes a difference. Verbally, some people are like bulls in china shops, rushing and roaring all over the place. From such we all need to be delivered!

Then consider the possibilities of the *written word*. Again, our words may not be clever but a short letter or notelet can have an effect out of all proportion to our expectations. The 'boss' who drops a line on the occasion of a birthday or the birth of a child may indicate an administration with a human face.

I read the autobiography of Lord Tonypandy—formerly George Thomas, a minister in a Labour government and then the greatly respected Speaker of the British House of Commons. He was a member of parliament for my home city for many years and as a young man I had been in touch with him. I was deeply moved by the memoirs of a fine man now retired and far from well and felt that I should write and tell him so. In reply, I had a handwritten letter which read as follows:

'It was a joy beyond measure for me to receive your
encouraging letter. I thank God for inspiring you to write
just when you did. Because my doctors place strict
limitations on the use of my voice (due to radium
treatment) I have long periods alone. My love of books and
writing keeps me going, but a letter like yours lights up the
sky for me.'

Frankly, I was humbled that a little note from me could mean so much and only glad that I had obeyed the impulse to write.

When I was a young man the national head of the organisation for which I worked had a pleasant habit of writing encouraging little notes to members of staff—usually, in lurid green ink and sometimes in a barely legible hand, particularly if he was writing while riding in a car. My friends and I sometimes smiled about those notes but it meant a lot that 'the big boss' took the trouble to send them, for all that. And whereas spoken words might have died in the air, the written words could remain in the pocket or on file for a long time as a recurring source of encouragement.

(There may be something in the idea of keeping a file of encouraging letters which we can turn to on days when nothing seems to be going right and 'all the angels appear to be flying in the wrong direction'.)

Sometimes, there may be a need for our written words to be put together for something beyond correspondence. We may need to write for newsletters or for the press. Referring to the printed alphabet, Benjamin Franklin said:

'Give me 26 lead soldiers and I will conquer the world'.

We may not conquer the world through our writing but we may still make a valuable contribution.

It would be good to realise that writing may be both an art and a craft and for those ready to learn there is an abundance of books and courses which are helpful. For many, the most difficult part is 'getting down to it', applying the seat of the pants to the seat of the chair! Most people find that for every modicum of inspiration in writing there must be the expenditure of much perspiration. So be warned!

Talking Without Boring

Then there is the *platform word*. People in many walks of life are likely to be asked to speak in public. During many years as a Rotarian I listened to hundreds of eminent people speak at club meetings. Some did an excellent job but with others it was painfully obvious that public speaking was just not 'their thing'.

It has been said that if all the people who fall asleep during after-dinner speeches could be put end to end—they'd be a lot more comfortable! It has also been remarked that while heresy may have slain its thousands boredom has slain its tens of thousands.

Of course preparation is essential and, strangely, sometimes a short talk may require as much preparation as a long one, if it is to be effective.

The speaker may need to prepare himself. I heard of a Jew who went through the holocaust and subsequently spoke publicly about his experiences on many occasions. He said that after a while he became so familiar with his speech that he ceased to feel quite as keenly the horrors of which he spoke. So, he made a practice of always getting to the venue at least an hour before the time for his talk so that he could feel his way back into the traumas through which he and his friends had passed.

If we get into the habit of speaking 'feelingly' about what we don't really feel then the perceptive people in the audience will soon recognise an act when they see one. On the other hand if we have a message about which we have real conviction that is likely to be communicated.

Those who speak frequently should be constantly looking for material and need to have a filing system to make sure that useful items don't escape the memory just when they are needed most.

Speakers should read themselves full, think themselves straight and then let themselves go!

It goes without saying that a speaker needs thoroughly to master his material including the quotes or stories designed to prevent attention from flagging. It is said that as a young man Winston Churchill used to stand in front of a mirror and 'practice his impromptus'. What seemed to be off the cuff comments had been studiously rehearsed in advance.

In preparation, some people write out full notes of what they want to say and that is a very useful discipline even if they memorise the substance of the notes or only have a skeleton outline with them when they 'stand and deliver'. Actually, each person must discover what is best for them in this respect.

Grabbing Attention

Not only is it necessary to prepare what is to be said but the way in which it is to be said. Special attention must be given to the opening remarks to ensure that they grab attention. For example, I have sometimes begun a talk by repeating 'the speaker's prayer':

> *'Lord, fill my mouth with all good stuff—and nudge me*
> *when I've said enough!'*

That has often evoked a fervent response, even from the irreligious!

But having grabbed attention it must then be retained. It has been said that if, after a reasonable time, a speaker doesn't strike oil he should stop boring! If he can't finish he can always stop. That's all very well, but if he is charged to deliver a serious message it may not be that simple.

In public speaking presentation is important. The tone of voice, gestures, body language, and especially eye-contact will make a difference. A speaker should always do his hearers the courtesy of looking at them. Some may have to drop their eyes occasionally to look at notes but the less that is necessary the better. Speakers on TV often give the impression of looking at the viewers even though they are reading from what is known as an auto cue. In public meetings we are unlikely to have that advantage.

It is important that what the speaker says is audible. If there is a microphone it may be possible to get close to it and speak softly, as long as the voice is not used explosively. Where there is no microphone it is necessary to lift the voice. In any case, articulation is important. Sometimes listeners may be able to hear a voice and not pick out the words being used because they are being mumbled or allowed to run into each other.

Most importantly, a public speaker must remember that what matters is not what he or she may get out of his or her head but what they manage to get into the heads of the hearers. Communication is the name of the game and words plus personality are the wonderful vehicles at our disposal.

Chapter Twenty-Three

Making an Impression

ELSEWHERE in this book I have written about winners making effective use of words but there are other ways in which, even unconsciously, we may make an impression. As a sometime wordsmith I might have been taken aback by the analysis of psychologist Albert Mehrabian who claimed that only 7 per cent of any message about our feelings and attitudes comes from the spoken words we employ. About 38 per cent comes from our tone of voice and 55 per cent from our facial expressions and, presumably, other 'body language'.

We walk into a room and, without realising it perhaps, something of what we are is conveyed. Our optimism may be reflected in our gait or our anxiety by the furrows on our brow. We may betray nervousness by our involuntary twitches or reveal confidence by the steady look in our eyes. What we are shows through more than we realise.

I recall an elderly housewife I knew in a little English village. I certainly mean no disrespect when I say that she was not particularly good looking. Nor was her dress anything but very ordinary. Yet a prominent local businessman said to me, 'That woman carries her goodness in her face!' Similarly, the former head of a leading Australian bank spoke to me about a retired man living in Melbourne. He said, 'That man always looks clean —inside and out!'

Much of the non-verbal impression we make upon other people will be involuntary and simply related to what we are, but to some extent we can check ourselves and guard against selling ourselves short.

First impressions can count a great deal. There may be a certain positive aura about us before people's critical faculties go to work dissecting and pigeon-holing us. Many factors may have a bearing—what we wear, our general demeanour, the timbre of our voice or our facial expression. There may be critical times when we need to monitor not only what we say but how we communicate in other ways.

For example, if we are going to address a meeting or apply for a job we need to make sure that our approach is suitable for the situation and a little prior research may be a good idea. There may be times when informal dress will give just the desired impression, whereas other situations may call for a different approach.

Appearance Counts

Like it or not, appearance can count. In some firms the fellow with the ragged jeans or the girl with huge, razzle dazzle ear-rings may fit in well whereas in other places their application for a job will be likely to go down like a lead balloon, regardless of their qualifications. There are organisations that regard dress code as important for their corporate image. Individualists may say that they want to be their own persons and that's fine, but unless they have strong overriding claims to acceptance they may have to conform if they want to be somebody else's employee. Tough? Yes, but that's the way it sometimes is.

A firm (but not vice-like) handshake can help. Eye contact is important. (I once conducted a rather disconcerting interview with an academic who persisted in looking at the ceiling or out of the window while he talked. He had nothing to hide but he certainly could have given the impression that he did.) A warm smile will be fine but a persistent, inane grin may do no good at all. Perhaps the most important thing is to be natural. Most people have difficulty with folk who are affected and stilted in their manner, and a facade is soon detected for what it is.

Thinking of impressions, it is often said that actions speak louder than words. And I would add that sometimes reactions speak even louder.

I recall a man speaking of an experience he had while a student at college. Apparently he had been late for a lecture and was running, head down, to the classroom. Rounding a corner he ran straight into his revered college principal, knocked him flat on his back, and then recoiled in horror at what he had done. He expected an explosion but instead the great man simply picked himself up, dusted himself down, bowed to the student, courteously wished him a good morning and went on his way. Knowing the said principal well (he conducted my wedding) I could easily envisage the scene and from what the fellow said I got the impression that that reaction was more telling than all the erudite lectures that the principal may have given.

In certain circumstances our reactions and the impression they leave may be critical. For example, in a job interview how do we react when a member of the selection panel seems to try and needle us? What about when an important client lodges a complaint and perhaps unjustly holds us responsible for something which has gone wrong?

It may be easy to create a good impression when everything is going our way but what about when it seems that there is a banana skin on every paving stone and we seem likely to slip at every corner? If we can give a good impression then we must be winners!

Chapter Twenty-Four

Practical Idealists

G.K. CHESTERTON contended that if you are looking for lodgings you should not only ask a landlady about such mundane matters as the rent and whether baths are included. You should enquire about her philosophy, on the understanding that if that is all right everything else will be fine!

In principle, that sounds good, but what about in practice? Sometimes, although not always, 'nice guys' have very distinctive and clearly defined philosophies or religious beliefs. It may be those beliefs which make them 'nice', but their philosophy and doctrine may seem so much 'mumbo jumbo' unless it is translated into the language of life and worked out amid the complexities of the real, hard world.

A speaker and writer who influenced me greatly as a young man was Albert Orsborn. I remember him saying:

> 'Many a beautiful ideal has been murdered by a gang of brutal facts'.

Too true! Yet, beautiful ideals are worth preserving for without them the world would be even more nasty and brutish than it sometimes is.

John is a man with very clearly defined religious beliefs. He joined a Melbourne advertising agency as a junior executive and finished up as managing director, owning 40 per cent of the shares in the company with its 52 million dollar annual turnover. At the outset he made clear that there were some accounts on which he wouldn't work and on which he would be very unconvincing anyway, because of his personal convictions.

He soon discovered that while some agencies might be prepared to be all things to all people and be controlled by the ethics of their clients those who were very ethical tended to be leaders in the field. For his company, John espoused a philosophy of seeking to identify for a client a unique selling benefit that was demonstrable.

Like most people in commerce John recognised that he was paid to be relevant to the public he served. In connection with a campaign against drinking and driving a slogan most favoured by a sample of the public contained a mild expletive which was not part of John's personal vocabulary. After some heart searching, John agreed to employ it and was encouraged that at least in part because of the campaign the road toll in the state of Victoria dropped by more than 50 per cent.

In employing people John had to seek the best professionals available who could espouse the general philosophy of the agency, whether or not they happened to share his particular personal beliefs. So, while his own ideals might affect the overall conduct of the company they could not dictate all the personal beliefs or conduct of individual staff members. It was necessary to maintain a balance between obligations to employees, shareholders and the public—and still be true to himself.

Ethical Considerations

Coming to terms with the possible while still striving for the ideal may be painful, but it is necessary. It would be nice if all choices were between black and white. Often they are between varying shades of grey and complicated by a variety of considerations.

At times people wrestle with ethical considerations concerning investments. In this respect, the organisation for which I worked for many years had certain 'no go' areas, enterprises with which we would not be involved. Fair enough, but without doubt there were times when, given the complexities of high finance, monies placed in a financial institution were re-invested in ways which were beyond our control and which might not have been to our liking.

Some companies have, on conscientious grounds, refused to invest in countries with repressive regimes. In some instances their policies have helped to topple dictatorships of one kind or another. But sometimes it may be that it has not been the juntas but the poorest of the poor who have suffered most from the lack of investment.

In recent years there has been an increased vigilance lest people in public life might have a conflict of interests and be liable to use their elected office and its influence in order to line their pockets. So be it. Those who legislate for others should be seen as 'squeaky clean' and not compromised in any way.

Malcolm Fraser, a former Prime Minister of Australia, said, 'Life wasn't meant to be easy'. Whatever it was meant to be, it certainly isn't a bed of roses for those who seek to balance idealism and realism.

Such a person was Dag Hammarskjold, a former Secretary General of the United Nations who died in the course of his duty for that organisation. He left a personal diary of meditations called *Markings* which is a classic in its way. In it, he wrote:

'In our era the road to holiness necessarily passes through the world of action'.

Many who might shy from using the word 'holiness' sincerely want to maintain integrity in what seems to be the jungle of life. They may have to bend but they don't want to break. They need to be flexible and yet still strong where principle is at stake.

Sometimes contemporaries can give guidance and sometimes not. We may have to take our direction from the stars rather than from the footprints in the shifting sand beneath our feet. In other words, we may have to rely on such general principles as are found, for example, in the Ten Commandments or the Sermon on the Mount. After all, they are always timely because they are timeless!

Chapter Twenty-Five

Getting Things Done

A LINE of an old pop song went: 'It's not what you do but the way that you do it'. That could have a much wider application than might be indicated by the song! For example, in effecting change in an organisation the process may be very important. I have known people who have introduced radical changes but in such a way that others have not felt threatened and have given full co-operation. Such leaders have taken time to carry judgement.

On the other hand there have been 'bosses' who have done the right things but in such a way that they've managed to ruffle many feathers in the process and have finished up with little more than grudging support, if not downright subversion.

There are folk who are ready to help but they are so patronising or off-hand in their manner that others are inclined to say, 'Forget it!'

I had occasion to visit a medical specialist—after a long wait for an appointment, be it said. I was hardly into the consulting room before I felt that the doctor was really too busy to be bothered. Now I appreciate that professional people can be under pressure —after all, I have led a very busy life myself—but if impatience with people shows through overmuch what is done for them may have a greatly reduced value. Winners should try to have winning ways of doing what has to be done.

When we do Things

Sometimes it is not so much a matter of the *way* we do things but *when* we do them that makes all the difference. In the people-business timing can be so important. Sometimes we speak of a 'word in season'—that is saying something that needs to be said but saying it at the right time. I am sure that, in common with others, I have often been way out in my timing but I recall one occasion at least when, remarkably, I got it right.

I was a young man living in London, England and had spent time in the reflection and meditation with which I like to start a day. Before eight o'clock in the morning I had an urge to call on a particular family. It seemed crazy. After all, I had seen the folk only the night before and the idea of an early morning social call didn't seem to make much sense. However, I responded to this nagging conviction and rode on my bicycle to where the family lived.

The door was opened by one of the younger children who said, 'Come in quickly, Mummy has just been taken ill'. The woman had seen her eldest son off to work and then collapsed. I am not a doctor but could see that the situation was serious and so I ran to a phone box and called an ambulance. In a very short space of time the woman was in hospital and an emergency operation was taking place. It was later stated that had there been any more delay she could not have survived. Interestingly, many years later I was in the same hospital as a patient and an unexpected visitor was the woman I had visited so long before.

Now I am not psychic and the experience I have cited was unusual, to say the least. I only refer to it as an example of the way in which the timing of what we do may sometimes be of the very essence. The right thing done at the wrong time may be of little use; it may even be disastrous. That is why it is important that we have our antennae out and are sensitive to situations and possible needs, if we are to be winners.

Why we do Things

But if the way we do things and when we do them is important *why* we do them may also make a difference. We should never underestimate the perceptiveness of people or their ability to suss out insincerity.

I guess that we all have mixed motives for many of the things we do. We may not always understand ourselves and the springs of action within us. Perhaps the last conceit we let go is the idea that we really know ourselves. Be that as it may, nice guys certainly try to be sincere in what they do. And it shows!

T.S. Eliot's play *Murder in the Cathedral is* based on the story of the slaying of Archbishop Thomas Becket in Canterbury Cathedral in AD 1170. It tells of four temptations which came to Becket. The first was to return to the follies of his youth. The second was to resume the powers of the chancellorship and the third to throw in his lot with the barons. These temptations were easily resisted but a fourth was of a more subtle and more dangerous kind. The Archbishop was tempted to seek the way of martyrdom for his own honour and glory.

This temptation too was overcome and described by Becket in the following lines:

> *Temptation shall not come in this kind again.*
> *The last temptation is the greatest treason,*
> *To do the right deed for the wrong reason.*

To do the right things for the right reason is to be a real winner —and that's a tall order for any of us.

Chapter Twenty-Six

Winners in Retirement

A LETTER from a fine old gentleman of over ninety made me think. He wrote, *'He who vegetates is lost'*. The Concise Oxford Dictionary indicates that to vegetate is to 'live an uneventful or monotonous life'.

So is that what retirement means? Is that all a person may get in return for those superannuation payments? Not according to my ninety year old friend who is still living adventurously, within the limits of physical frailty. He has no intention of wasting the extra golden years given to him by providence and through advances in medical science.

R.L. Stevenson—a winner in many ways—wrote:

> *'Even if the doctor does not give you a year, even if he hesitates about a month, make one brave push and see what can be accomplished in a week...To travel hopefully is better than to arrive, and the true success is to labour'.*

Brave words from a man who suffered from much sickness!

As a child I was taught 'the three Rs'—reading, (w)riting and (a) rithmetic. Now I am learning the fourth 'R'—retirement, and it certainly doesn't mean vegetating.

Of course, retirement means different things for different people. One woman said that for her it meant half as much money and twice as much husband! I heard a man facing retirement say that for the first six months he just intended to sit in his rocking chair. After that he would start to rock a little. He was only joking!

By way of contrast, I have heard of some retirees in one country who, with tongue in cheek, I imagine, speak of 'growing old disgracefully'. As far as I know they don't get into real mischief but apparently are into all sorts of unlikely pursuits like riding big motorcycles, for example. As people are living longer so 'grey power' is becoming an increasing factor in politics and a pressure group which cannot be ignored.

For some, retirement is a shining gateway; for others it is a black hole. Some are only too glad to be released from the burden of responsibility; others feel diminished on becoming retirees. I heard one man say that the day before retirement he felt like a rooster; the day after he felt like a feather duster!

The state of health may well affect feelings. If people are unwell the prospect of more leisure may be especially attractive. If there is the finance to ensure a reasonable standard of living after retirement, anxiety may be eased.

For some the prospect of spending more time with their family may give retirement special appeal. (After years of separation from them my wife and I are getting to know our grandchildren better and being educated in the process, I may say!)

Going Stale?

Some regard the day of their retirement as their 'use by date' and allow themselves to go stale thereafter, feeling that their usefulness is finished. I knew a man who almost literally spent the last five years of his life looking out of a window for this reason.

On the other hand I have known people who have pushed themselves too hard in retirement, forgetting that their physical strength could hardly be expected to be what it may have been in their youth. Clearly, the aim should be to achieve a sensible balance.

It may be wise to prepare for retirement both mentally and financially. This should not mean 'putting down our barrow' prematurely or shutting off enthusiasm for our tasks before time.

It should mean preparing positively for what can be a new and positive phase of our lives. Many enlightened firms now arrange seminars to help staff with retirement in view.

An unknown prankster in the office building where I worked put an unauthorised statement on the official notice board. It read:

> *'Owing to the present economic situation the light at the end of the tunnel will be turned off until further notice'.*

Winners wouldn't buy that idea. They believe that the best is always yet to be, even in retirement.

To win in retirement I believe that it is necessary to take an interest in the world around. So many exciting things are happening. We can look to the world of nature—the woods, the fields, the garden or even the window box. We can consider the world of technology. I have spoken to retirees who have been fascinated to explore the wonders of computers and have discovered new horizons for themselves. Then current affairs in the country and in the world can be absorbing and, thanks to modern media, we can keep in touch with what is happening.

Small Parcels?

To be winners in retirement we must have concern for other people. Folk who are wrapped up in themselves make very small parcels! If we are merely concerned about ourselves life will be likely to shrivel and diminish but in doing things for others we will also be helping ourselves to stay happy and healthy.

I deplore any sort of apartheid based on age. While understanding that different age groups are likely to have different perceptions and separate interests, I believe that they also have something to give to each other. I believe that young folk sometimes take more notice of what older people say than they might care to admit—particularly when the elderly are not censorious but tactfully helpful and understanding of the rapidly changing world in which we live. At the same time, elderly people can be stimulated by the energy and interest of the young.

I frequently visit a retirement village where many of the residents are active in maintaining the amenities and activities.

"To win in retirement.......it is necessary to take an interest...."

They tend the gardens and organise painting classes, outings, study groups, bowls and other sports. They visit each other and share shopping and other necessary chores—while still respecting each other's independence and right to privacy. As a result, for most there is never a dull moment. We all have a need to be needed and, paradoxically, through forgetting ourselves we find ourselves and discover that that need is met.

It is important to have aims and objectives for each day and for the longer term. We need to have good reason to get up and get on with living. Some will find such reason on the golf course or with a fishing rod and line. Others will be motivated through their membership of a club or a church. All may find that the real prizes are within themselves—fulfilment, faith, contentment and a sense of self-worth. Such prizes are not merely for a select few; they are for us all.

> *Age is a quality of mind:*
> *If you have left your dreams behind,*
> *If hope is cold;*
> *If you no longer look ahead,*
> *If your ambition's fires are dead,*
> *Then you are old!*
> *But if from life you take the best*
> *And if in life you keep the jest,*
> *If love you hold -*
> *No matter how the years go by,*
> *No matter how the birthdays fly,*
> *You are not old!*

Chapter Twenty-Seven

The End is the Beginning

SUCCESS may be not so much a destination as a journey, not merely static but dynamic and ongoing. To an extent, success (or failure) is within us; it's what we do with what happens to us. Michel Quoist said:

'My only reason for being on earth is to work at becoming'.

We may have sometimes seen 'winning' as making a lot of money or reaching a certain position and, without doubt, both achievements can bring satisfaction and increase feelings of self-worth. But we may soon need to ask how well we can use the money when we've made it? What will we do in the coveted position when we have attained it? Will we make a success of our successes and build on them or fail to turn them to good account?

If we feel that we have arrived and can lean on our oars then drifting will be inevitable. If we feel that there are no more worlds to conquer then we'll soon be dead—even if we don't actually lie down!

It seems that to live zestfully human beings need to have elusive horizons, peaks that beckon, challenges that stir and stimulate.

Sometimes the challenges will come unbidden; life itself will throw down the gauntlet. At other times we will have to lift our eyes and seek for that which will call up the best from within us. We may have to climb out of the groove which can so easily become a grave and, with the wind in our faces, make for higher ground.

"*What will we do in the coveted position when we have attained it?*"

Dietrich Bonhoeffer, the German mystic hanged by the Nazis at the end of the second World War, said that every apparent end could be a more glorious new beginning. Nice guys had better believe it.

As we reach the conclusion of this book it will have failed in its purpose if writer and readers alike are not motivated to make the rest of their lives the best of their lives. Hopefully, some phrase, at least, will have helped to serve that end.

Further Reading
From Wrightbooks

The Joy of Winning by Michael Beer

A completely different 'success' book, it shows that to be a winner you don't have to be a superman—that you need no special aptitude, education, intelligence or character. You will learn that you can win without turning your life upside-down.

Assert Yourself by Robert Sharpe

This is a book for all those who believe that they could, and should, get a better deal in their social and working lives. All they need is a little help and advice—especially when it comes to standing up for themselves, or their rights, in situations which they feel to be awkward or embarrassing.

Believe You Can! by Allen Carmichael

This book has been written to make you think. To think about yourself, about the person you are now and about the person you really want to be. To show you how to create self-awareness and build a new self-image. To encourage you to walk tall, acquire a sense of your own value and total uniqueness and, above all, to believe in your ability to alter circumstances.

Winning People Over by Michael Beer

Important though self-motivation may be, success in life often comes through success in motivating others, bringing them onside, getting them to see things your way—winning them over.